MARKETING FOR PEOPLE WHO THINK THEY DON'T DO MARKETING—If you want a road map to creating a simple but effective marketing plan for your business, this is it. Written in a simple, familiar, breezy, and funny style, this book demystifies the process of establishing, selling, and maintaining your brand and is stuffed full of excellent advice. The highest recommendation I can give is this: I'm an artist. I hate sales and I hate marketing, but this book made me go, "Oh. That's what it is. That's how it works. I guess marketers really aren't evil after all and it's not as hard as I thought it would be." If you're selling something, this book will teach you how to get people to buy it. *–Jon Bastian*

LEARN TO GO FROM CHAOS TO ORDER—If you want to learn anything in this field, Hank is your teacher. *–Mel Powell*

SIMPLY PRACTICAL—This is an excellent book, full of useful tips and insights about marketing. If you own your own business, you'll find many useful examples and ideas to take your business to the next level. Best yet: there's no marketese speak here. The ideas are easy to understand and easy to implement. *—Dan Janal*

As executive director of a non-profit foundation, marketing and fundraising is always a unique challenge. I attended one of Yuloff's marketing seminars and quickly learned how much I needed to learn. So, I anxiously awaited the release of this book. I now have my Marketing Bible. Great ideas, great suggestions! *—Kathleen Hale*

A MUST-READ MARKETING BOOK! Yet another fabulous marketing book from Hank & Sharyn Yuloff! Their tips & ideas on effective social media marketing are excellent. So glad I bought this book! *—Cynthia Lay*

GREAT MARKETING TIPS—There's always room for improvement on marketing your message as a business owner. Hank and Sharyn Yuloff make it fun and easy to up your game and focus on what works. —*Wil Bowers*

ANSWERS ALL YOUR QUESTIONS! Excellent! Clear! Pertinent! Helpful! And, entertaining! If you are floundering and want a way to tackle social media, THIS IS YOUR BOOK! —*Joia Jitahidi*

Great Book! I have been in the marketing field so some of this stuff I already knew, but even with my experience I picked up quite a few nuggets that I've already implemented into my business. —*Jack Stone*

This is a smart book for anyone looking for a working proven system for success. —*Craig A. Valine*

I was absolutely thrilled when I learned Hank Yuloff had penned this book. He did a brain dump of his three decades of marketing knowledge. A business owner or independent contractor would be foolish not to have this marketing bible on their desk. Hank has made it easy for you to apply strategies that flat out work. This is a solid HOW TO! Don't pass this one up. You can't afford NOT to own this book. —*Joseph Buzello*

WONDERFUL BOOK WITH COUNTLESS TIPS TO BOOST YOUR BUSINESS—I applied just a couple of tips and I'm receiving more clients. —*Nargas*

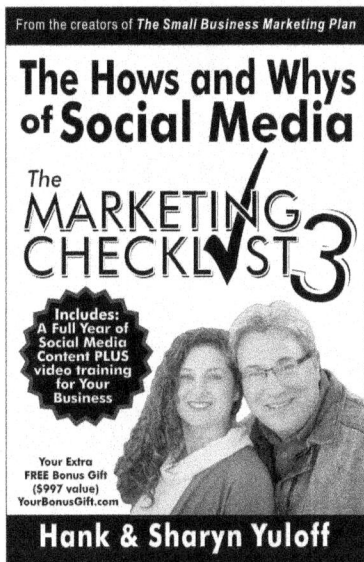

THE MARKETING CHECKLIST FOR SALES

THE MARKETING CHECKLIST FOR SALES

49 Easy Ways to Improve Your Sales

for Professionals Who Don't Like Selling

Hank and Sharyn Yuloff

Naked Book Publishing

can generally expect from the information. No representation in any part of this information materials and/or seminar training are guarantees or promises for actual performance. Any statements, strategies, concepts, techniques, exercises and ideas in the information, materials and/or seminar training offered are simply opinion or experience, and thus should not be misinterpreted as promises, typical results or guarantees (expressed or implied). The author and publisher (Henry "Hank" Yuloff, Sharyn Yuloff, Naked Book Publishing nor any of their representatives) shall in no way, under any circumstances, be held liable to any party (or third party) for any direct, indirect, punitive, special, incidental or other consequential damages arising directly or indirectly from any use of books, materials and/or seminar trainings, which is provided "as is," and without warranties.

PRINTED IN THE UNITED STATES OF AMERICA

Contents

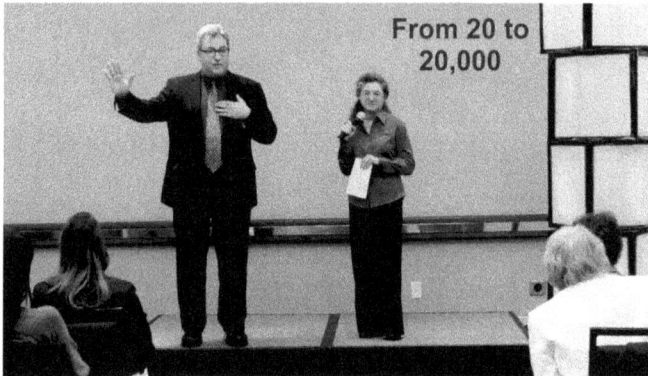

We would like to welcome you to the fifth addition to *The Marketing Checklist* series of business books. Like the other books this one is made up of a combination of reworked, updated, and edited blog posts as well as original content created to match the subject matter of the book.

We continue to add to this series of books because we know that you, our audience members, have a sincere desire to improve your businesses and we are here to help you.

Please email info@YuloffCreative.com, if you have questions about the content, and we will do our best to answer. Put "Book Content Question" in the subject line.

If you would like to book us to speak to your business group, you can send an email to info@YuloffCreative.com and put "Speak to Our Group" in the subject line. We have limited days each year but love to educate small business owners on the latest in marketing, human resources, sales, and public speaking.

Prologue

The Wheelbarrow and the Gold Coins

A few years ago, we were fortunate enough to be speaking on stage at the same event as Brian Tracy (yes, that Brian Tracy!) Wait, you don't know who Brian Tracy is? Please look him up—your future self will thank you! This was one of over two hundred days a year when Brian was on stage, teaching sales and speaking, and I must have taken a dozen pages of notes. I was in active learning mode because "if you are not learning, you are not earning."

After the morning session, the speakers got to have lunch with Brian. We thought that this was going to be an even *better* opportunity to learn from Brian Tracy up close. Sharyn and I got to the restaurant in the hotel and made sure we were seated at the same table with Brian. We had questions at the ready. During the salad course, we noticed something. Brian was asking the other people at the table questions. *And*, he was taking notes, capturing information he would use in his presentation—golden nuggets.

After lunch, all 350 of us, guests and speakers, were back in the second-floor ballroom. But as we got started, noise began coming up from the pool area one floor below. There was an end of summer party going on. And it was loud. As I sat in the second row, looking up at Brian Tracy, I thought if anyone had earned the right to go ballistic (you know, I-can't-work-in-situations-like-this kind of ballistic) it would be Brian. But then, he walked to the front of the stage, leaned toward us as if sharing a secret, and said something that would forever change how I act when we are on stage. He gave me a *forever golden nugget*.

Imagine this: You wake up super early on a beautiful spring Sunday morning in Sedona, Arizona. Those mornings somehow seem magical, right? You make your coffee and decide to pour it into a travel mug to take a bit of a drive. You point your car towards the mountains and enjoy the fresh breeze on your arm and the left side of your face. The sun's just coming up, so the breeze is still a little cool. It doesn't take you long to arrive at the base of your closest mountain. You drive just little bit higher and you come to a trail head. The sign says that there are caves. Caves are always fun to explore, right?

You lean against the car, feeling the warmth of the engine on your rear, and finish the last of your coffee. You lock up the car and walk a bit along the trail. It isn't long before you find the first cave entrance. You notice something glistening along the floor of the cave. Using the flashlight feature of your smartphone, you shine it in front of you and notice the ground is layered with gold coins. Holy cow! You look around to see if anyone is watching, which, of course, no one is. You quickly gather as many of the coins as you can carry in your shirt, but there are so many more. You take off your shoes and fill your socks with coins. You carry all the coins back to your car, knowing that there are more in the cave.

"If only," you think, "I had a shovel and a wheelbarrow." Of course, you could drive the ninety minutes to a big box store and buy them. But how much do those cost? Weighing the time and expense you decide, in the end, to be happy with the coins you have and head back down the hill, down to where you're comfortable. Down to the comfort of your home.

This is how we find that many entrepreneurs feel about coaching; instead of focusing on the golden nuggets, they are worried about the cost of the shovel and wheelbarrow. Instead of investing in their business, they are busy just trying to do more of what they were taught to do.

But that's not you, right? We know that because you have committed to growing your business by investing time and money reading this book, (and perhaps attending The Small Business Breakthrough Bootcamp!) And after you finish this book (and bootcamp), you won't just go back down the hill to where it's comfortable. Not you. You will use everything you learn to build your business into something that is bigger and better.

We look forward to welcoming you and helping you in every way we can! We'll fill your wheelbarrow with lots of *golden nuggets*.

1

Marvin Says, "It All Starts with an Elevator"

We were about to speak to 150 business owners about social media and the best way to build your business. As I got dressed, I needed to pick a tie. A tie that would somewhat coordinate with Sharyn's maroon shirt. From the bottom of the stack, a tie that I had not worn in years spoke to me.

"Wear me."

Wear you?

"Yes—if you wear me, I *promise* something great will happen."

Okay, I believed in ties and they have never lied to me, so I grabbed it and *goodness*, it was a tie with Mickey Mouse on it that says, "It All Started with a Mouse."

It all started with a mouse. I thought about that for a bit. Walt Disney originally had a mouse with a different name. He changed it to Mickey. And drawings became cartoons. And that turned into one of the most popular brands in the world.

That made me think of something else.

Years ago, Sharyn and I were asked to participate in a group called the New Leaders Project where up and coming entrepreneurs were taught what it is like to be part of leadership in the community. We met lots of other businesspeople our age, and lots of leaders in positions we aspired to be in.

One of them was retired Los Angeles City Councilman, Marvin Braude. Never heard of him? That's okay. What you must know about Mr. Braude is that it is because of him you can eat in a restaurant and almost everywhere else without being disturbed by nasty cigarette smoke.

One day, Mr. Braude was in an elevator with a pregnant woman; several other people who were all smoking. She coughed and Braude thought, there really should be a law that would prevent people from being forced to inhale smoke. Then he thought, "I am an LA city councilman. I can *write* that law."

3

He did and it spread from there. Soon, there were laws establishing non-smoking areas and finally, the only smoking area for Los Angeles was Las Vegas.

As Mr. Braude was speaking to us, he said that his message was simple. You can have a huge goal. But sometimes, what you need to do is start small. You can start with an elevator.

Let's talk about *your* elevator.

Do you have an elevator? Do you have a goal? A project you need to start? What ideas to you have that you have not acted upon? When are you getting started?

Do you have some goals where you have not even taken a first step in the direction of those goals? Is it because they are so large that you are frozen by inaction? We have all seen the expression, "A journey of a thousand miles starts with a single step." It is supposed to tell us to just take that first step. Which, sure, is easy, but not when we keep looking waaaaaaaay down the road a thousand miles ahead.

We have a project. Four actually. And, they are all books.

The first one came during a break in mastermind session when I had a conversation with Dan Janel. Dan's business is helping first time authors go from idea to publication of their first book. He told me that, "I read your book *The Marketing Checklist 2* and think that you and Sharyn should write a book about couples who work together."

That was a lightbulb moment and twenty-four hours later, Sharyn and I came up with a title, a cover design, bought the URL, and created a list of questions that we would need to answer as chapters. Our first steps were taken, but there are many more. We need to find between five and ten couples who want to be part of the book (we think that it would be better to have several points of view) and are willing to invest in becoming best-selling authors. Or we need to write the entire book ourselves. So, while we're creating the process to look for couples, or deciding to do it ourselves, we are stuck. That and we need to find a teeter-totter for the front cover photo.

Another project we have is a book about how the laws of physics can be used to describe how to market your business. For *that* book, we are waiting for our co-author, Randy Gold, to write the physics part. Then we will write the marketing laws that tie in. For example, Newton's first law of motion states that (roughly, remember, I am not writing that part) a body in motion will stay in motion until acted upon by an outside force. The marketing equivalents? Your marketing is going to continue to suck until you do something to change it. Well, it may end up more graceful than that.

Then there are two more books in *The Marketing Checklist* series. One is a marketing tips book, and the other is a sales tip book.

Each of these books has a checklist of things we need to do for them to be completed.

For your goals you need to do the same thing. Write them down so that you can assess at any moment, how far along you are in your journey. You will not be overwhelmed or overconfident that the project will be completed.

This is especially important for the products you are selling. (Were you wondering when I would get to sales?) It is so important to "checklist your process," It will make it easy to follow up and follow through. Your clients can also benefit from your checklist because it allows them to see your progress and realize that you are there to assist them in their business.

Remember this most important of sales rules: 99.999% of people in the world do *not* want to write you a check. The good news is that .001% would keep you very busy. Your job as a salesperson, or as the owner of a company looking for new clients, is to solve their problems. If you take away your client's pain, you will receive their support and their money.

Sales is not about you. It is about *them*. You can say you care, but until you demonstrate it, the sales will not happen. All you must do is help them ride their elevator without being disturbed by cigarette smoke.

Do you want help in finding your elevator, or helping your clients find theirs? Let's have a conversation. Go to www.FreeMarketingConsulation.com and after you answer a few easy questions, you can choose a time in our calendar that is best for you. *Ding!* Your elevator doors have opened. It's time to rise to the top. All you must do is step in and we can help you. Will you let us?

2

Why It's Easier to Sell to the Three Bears Than Goldilocks

We are all familiar with Goldilocks and the three bears. Goldilocks does a B&E into the bears home, falls asleep in their bed, and almost takes a shot from a nine-millimeter as she runs out the door.

But let's look at this from a marketing point of view.

Goldilocks *clearly* had the better public relations department. We know this because we know *her* name, and not the bears. And her ending was kept out of the papers.

But if we want to advertise to the parties involved in this story, we know *a lot* more about the bears than Goldilocks.

The bears are a family of three. We know that their ages (in human equivalent) approximate early thirties for the parents and between eight and twelve for the child. We don't know if they are married because they sleep in separate beds. (Or, one of the adults has sleep apnea.)

They are big into family activities outdoors, like taking a walk in the woods.

They enjoy handmade furniture, and they are not opposed to eating a purely vegetarian meal, i.e., porridge.

They live in a rural area, not downtown, and do not have a house alarm.

We no virtually nothing about Goldilocks.

So, what is the point?

When you are promoting your company, you need to know your target markets so that when you use advertising, public relations, and branding your marketing messages will be more affective.

Would you like your *own* fairy tale ending for your business? If yes, go to FreeMarketingConsultation.com and take our brief assessment. Then click on the calendar link and you will receive a free thirty-minute focus call.

3

How to Get More Clients

No matter what we do, everyone in business has the same challenge—how do we get more clients.

The steps to get more clients have a very specific vocabulary: revenue goals, forecasts, prospect lists, reports, proposals, follow up, scripts, *effective* scripts, and the very worst—cold calling.

These terms are almost universally dreaded by every one of my clients. When we begin to talk about how to get more clients, and I bring up the subject of sales, my Universal Truth of Sales comes up:

> We have all been taught how to *do* what we do, but almost
> without exception, we are never taught how to get more clients
> by the people who teach us.

Let's talk about how to get more clients in eight steps.

The most important *first step* is this one: To start, I only want you to do it twenty-two minutes at a time. Just twenty-two minutes. Roughly the length of a thirty-minute comedy show on television if you remove the commercials. See? That's not so hard. But in return for just twenty minutes, you have to put your best foot forward for that time. No bathroom breaks or any other distractions.

The next step is to create a list. Let's make it a short list—twenty-five to fifty—of prospects that you think could be a consistent user of your product or a referral source. If fifty is too high, I'll let you get away with twenty-five. (Hey, it's *your* business. I'm just the voice in your head giving you marketing advice.) These must be solid choices. Take your time and make this list great. Each person on your list must fit your target market. If you need assistance with creating your target, I suggest you grab a copy of *The Small Business Marketing Plan* and fast forward to the beginning of day two.

The third step is to contact each person on your list. This is going to take time. You will not get through immediately to everyone. In fact, it is going to take a lot of effort. This third step is why people hate it when I tell them that everyone is in sales. Hatred of rejection. But here is the secret to getting more clients through sales: It's just numbers. More calls equals more sales. If you want those numbers to be fewer, you have to get better in sales skills. That is what the next few steps are for.

Step four is to get them to answer the phone and take your call.

Step five: When they say hello, your first response is to ask for a moment of their time. If they say no, let them know you will call back another time. Most likely they will ask who you are.

That is when you move to step six—the introduction call.

Step six is your ten-second reason for them to take your call. Your unique sales proposition (USP). It's your biggest benefit to them. (The USP is covered in day two of *The Small Business Marketing Plan*.) Let them know that you will be forwarding additional information and ask if it would be alright for you to follow up shortly thereafter. Most will say, "yes," but some may say, "no". That is *their* problem, not yours.

Your job after the phone call is, as soon as possible, to send them an interesting email or snail mail, perhaps an awesome promotional product, so that you begin to stand apart from all your many competitors. It is beyond crucial that you become memorable so that you are top of mind when the need arises.

Step seven is a face-to-face meeting for a sales presentation. Let me boil that part down to the basics:

- Ask questions designed to gain insight into how your product will solve their problems.
- Listen more than you speak.
- Tell the truth.
- Ask for the sale.

Step eight: repeat the entire process over and over, twenty minutes a day. When you can do twenty minutes easily, then increase it to twenty-nine minutes. Why twenty-nine? Simple, psychologically, I don't want you to think that it is a half hour. It *isn't*. It's just twenty-nine minutes. But you still can't go to the bathroom.

These are the basics of how to get more clients. We may be in different industries, but we all have the same challenges.

When you need help in the process, get in touch with us at Yuloff Creative

Marketing Solutions, either through the website or call us at 800-705-4265. You can also get a free marketing assessment at www.FreeMarketngConsultation.com . After you take it, you will be sent right into our calendar where we can talk about how to get more clients, or any other marketing challenges.

4

How to Find the Right Salesperson for Your Business

When people ask me how to find the right salesperson, I know it is going to be quite a conversation. Commission sales has been my primary occupation since I was in college. Even though our company has evolved into more of a service business, where we provide business coaching, focused on teaching you to create your marketing path, build your team, and how to get more business, I still hold true to the mantra that no matter what you and I do for a living we are all in sales. Your receptionist is the first salesperson a potential client speaks to, so he or she better know what you do, how you do it, and how to promote the company.

Here are the first *ten* questions I am going to ask when I want to find the right salesperson. This first section should take about *twenty* minutes maximum and will give me the outline of the prospect as a salesperson. If the answers are great, we will move on to the more creative section. One can even ask these questions in a phone pre-interview prior to meeting face-to-face.

- What does sales mean to you? (Let's see what they think of being in sales.)
- How did you decide to get into sales? (Rather than that "tell me about yourself" question.)
- What interested you about us? Why do you want to sell for us? (I want to see what research they did into our company. *If, at any time,* a prospect uses the phrase, "Sales is sales, it does not matter what I am selling," then this is the wrong person. This person will be job hopping, chasing each bright shiny object.)
- What was your average sale in previous jobs? (If your product cost $9997 and they are used to selling $500 products, this is going to be a huge jump in asking for the sale.)
- What was the average sales cycle? (Let's see how long the person had

to follow up on sales.)

- What do you think of sales quotas? How do you use them to motivate you?
- How do you prospect? (I want to see what kind of sales tools are used.)
- What is your last sales manager going to tell me about you when I call?
- Do you consider sales a career? (90% will say "*yes*," which allows you to ask the next question.)
- How do you improve yourself as a salesperson? (Let's see what kind of continuing education they are getting.)

So, by now, I am going to know if I like the person sitting in front of me for the job we have open. Those first *ten* questions will give me an idea if I want to continue. If not, do your best wrap up. If yes, move on to these next questions.

- Tell me about your best sale, ever. Followed by:
  * Where did the lead come from?
  * What was your first step towards the sale?
  * How did you feel when they said, "*yes?*"
  * How did you follow up after the sale?
  * Did you ask for referrals from them?
- Is that your most creative sale, ever? (Let's see if he wants to tell me about past sales. A great salesperson will have a lot of these stories.)
- Did you ever make a sale and wish you hadn't made it? (I'm searching for honesty. Allowing them to think about their past. They will never have heard this question, unless it was from someone else who read this.)
- How did your previous company obtain sales leads?
- If I asked to look at your calendar while you sold for another company, what would I see? (This question goes along with my theory that if most salespeople were arrested and charged with being a salesperson, there would not be enough evidence to convict them. A calendar that is mostly blank will make the viewer snow blind because there is so much white paper without anything on it.)
- What percentage of your presentations turned into sales? (This is going to vary by industry. Anywhere between 20% and 80% is normal, depending on the industry. What I am looking for here, is do they know their numbers and how do they present them to you.)

- In *six* months, what about you is going to tell me, "Wow, I am so glad I hired _____?" (Let's see if she plans on being with us that long and if she has a plan for success.)
- What kind of customer relationship tracking system did you use at past jobs?
- How do you define success?
- The last few questions are to throw them off guard just a bit and see how they think on their bum.
- Do you think this interview has been a success? (The standard answer will be, "It depends, are you hiring me?" Your answer is the next question.)
- How are you going to close me?
- Do you have any questions for me? What have I forgotten to ask you?

The final question will let you know for sure if this is the right person: *How are you going to follow up with this interview?*

This question will probably catch them off guard. You are looking for something more than the standard thank-you email. I want to see if they have a bit of a sense of humor as well. "I am thinking of sending you flowers, so I will need to know how your favorite bouquet is composed." The best answer would be for them to mention two or three different methods of connecting with you: email, handwritten note, phone call, connect on a social media platform. This shows they are used to doing the same thing with a prospect.

Finding the right salesperson is not an easy process. They don't do what you do, but they must be able to sell what you do. For example, if you hire a salesperson to bring business into your law or dental practice, they are not a lawyer or dentist. If you hire them to bring business into your auto body shop, they are not technicians who fix car bodies. You are hiring someone who is going to have to tell your story in an interesting way and make someone know, love, and trust you. They are going to have to understand that the average sale takes between five and twelve touches. They are going to have to put up with people saying, "no," and, "I need more information," without feeling let down.

You can make your job easier by making the ads you run as clear as possible as to what the salesperson is going to be selling and what they are going to be doing to sell your product. You can give them an honest expectation of the income level they can reach and the amount of time it will take to get there. A well written ad will make your entire process easier.

If you need assistance in learning how to interview salespeople, head to www.FreeMarketingConsultation.com. We will go over how you advertise and interview your new team members.

5

Success and the Underappreciated Salesperson—Ten Tips to Keep Your Top-Shelf Salespeople

We had an initial coaching call with a client this morning. He is a sharp businessperson and a leader in his industry and had been selling for a company for a while. Since I have been in that industry for thirty years we were able to connect quickly.

He said his biggest challenge was feeling that he was not doing a great job for his company.

Let's get to the point quickly, I thought, and asked what his volume was.

Wow. I've been in the top 20% or so in personal sales in the promotional products business for over two decades and his number was *double* mine.

"Let me get this straight," I asked. "You are writing that much business and you are feeling underappreciated?"

Knowing the profit margins for the industry, the volume he is generating should have allowed the company to hire a dedicated assistant for this salesperson and let him do his thing – create *tons* and *tons* of business. It turns out that since his business had dropped a bit last year from the previous one and he fell below an arbitrary number that the company had set for one to have a dedicated assistant available to them, he would now have to share.

Bad move. Especially when that salesperson starts talking to a marketing oracle and that marketing oracle fans the embers which have been lit in his head. Yes, that company has competitors and those competitors know *exactly* how to treat a salesperson of this caliber.

How does this happen? I think that it is a matter of complacency. This company has more than three-hundred salespeople and is viewing them all equally. The rules must apply equally or the bottom 90% of the group will be pissed.

So, here are *ten* tips for employers who have and want to keep your top-shelf salespeople:

1. All salespeople are not equal. Remember that.
2. Set up rules for how salespeople will be treated and follow them. Include in those rules an understanding that salespeople are very different from hourly employees. Incentives drive them.
3. Be transparent in showing how the rules are being put into play.
4. If you say that when a salesperson hits the certain dollar level, let's say the million-dollar mark for example, certain benefits will be added. Add the one-bad-year clause so that the salesperson feels that they have a safety net and that the company understands that sales can be tricky some years and if they stumble, the company has their back. That would help the sales rep who had a year of $850,000 and suddenly got stressed. This is especially helpful if you are in an industry, using this dollar amount example again, where the average was only $150,000. Why lose an $850,000 rep who is worth five average reps, just because they had a weird year?
5. Ask for input. If you are a sales-driven company, and which companies aren't, let your salespeople kick in their ideas on where the company is going. A company we work with, SendOutCards, has what they call the Eagles Nest, a group of top producers that changes each *six* months. The ownership has them on weekly calls to ask for advice and it has boosted sales tremendously.
6. "Appreciation wins out over self-promotion every time." Make sure you *tell* your salespeople, especially the top ones, you appreciate what they are doing and if they have issues, address them right away. When you have meetings, have the top salespeople on stage, sharing their success stories. If you have a salesperson who is not in the top level but still had a great sale, put *them* on stage to talk about that sale. It shows everyone what happens when they get to the top level.
7. Under promise and over deliver. Every now and then, have surprise incentives pop up that your salespeople have already won! "Surprise, we had a great month, so as a thank you, I'm sending everyone a gift card for . . . ."
8. Remember that everyone in the company can be in sales. Come up with a couple of programs which let the non-salespeople be part of the fun.
9. Survey your clients. When they say something great about their salesperson, let *everyone* know. If it is negative, ask the salesperson if the two of you need to come up with a plan to get that client back on your company's good side.

10. Don't be afraid to say "yes" but have the courage to say "no." Okay, some salespeople can be prima donnas. Be honest, show appreciation, and have them come up with a way that the *no* can be turned in to a *yes*.

These are just a few tips. I hope they help your company. If you need more help working with your sales team, give us a call at 800-705-4265.

6

What Kevin Harrington of *Shark Tank* Taught Us about Creating Third-Party Validation

Suppose you owned a car detailing company and had the opportunity to go shine Air Force One? That is, to me, an incredible third-party validation, celebrity endorsement for that industry, right? Not many detailers get that chance (I can only liken it to getting to detail Jay Leno's collection). We had chatted with them prior to them doing the work on how to leverage the opportunity from the event.

Do you think you would post a few (dozen) photos of you doing that job? After the event, we checked their website to see the coverage. We found— nothing! There was one tiny little mention that they were trained by a guy who has detailed AF1.

Even if they were not allowed to post pix of them doing the work, there should be a photo of the plane with a notation of when they got to work on it.

Everybody, opportunities like this do *not* happen all the time. When they *do*, you must *grab* them and use them to build your business.

We recently met with (and were interviewed by) Kevin Harrington, an original shark on *Shark Tank*, and he talked about the five different types of third-party validation testimonials and endorsements you can achieve. In order of ascending awesomeness they are:

- Consumer third-party validation testimonials
- Professional third-party validation testimonials
- Celebrity third-party validation testimonials
- Editorial third-party validation testimonials
- Clinical third-party validation testimonials

Consumer Testimonials

This is the testimonial that is the most common. You get them from your clients. Any testimonial is great and it's a way to highlight your clients as well.

When you get these endorsements use their entire name not only their initials. It's much better to have Hank Yuloff of Sedona, Arizona say that you are great than H.Y. of Sedona. Even *better* is to have those testimonials on video.

Professional Testimonials

This is when one of your industry colleagues gives you a testimonial on how you are doing in the world you share. As an example, Kay Wallace, social media and digital marketing expert, gave us this testimonial for our latest book which was a primer on social media, *The Marketing Checklist for Social Media Marketing: The Hows and Whys of Social Media:*

> When it comes to marketing your business and making your
> business successful, you better *be* an expert or hire one. And
> when it comes to *hiring* experts, Sharyn and Hank Yuloff are the
> #1 business and marketing team that should get your call. They
> always over deliver. This book is a great example. There are a
> bunch of books on social media platforms, but how many offer
> you a free year of social media *content* with them? Knowing the
> Yuloffs like I do, that content will grow and grow. Whether you
> are new to online marketing or use it every day, *The Marketing
> Checklist for Social Media Marketing* will raise your knowledge
> level and help you achieve more. Take advantage of their offers
> and you will catapult your business.

Celebrity Testimonials

When you can get a celebrity to give you a testimonial, that is grand. They may not have the professional pizzazz, but their kind words give you solid third-party validation. We have been fortunate to have **Dave Pratt, owner of Star Worldwide Networks and a Radio Hall of Fame member**, give us testimonials for our last two books. His style is pure fun:

> When a major league baseball player is asked how to hit a
> 100-mph breaking ball, he will likely say something like, "Keep
> your eyes open and get ahead of the curve." The same is true for
> today's media as it moves fast and is constantly changing. You
> need to stay ahead of the curve, or you will definitely strike out.
> Hank and Sharyn are in your coaches' box, spitting sunflower
> seeds and barking out encouragement from the dugout. Social
> media is dominant today, but you must understand how to
> inject your social platforms with steroids. You need the compet-
> itive edge. Millions of people have played Little League, but few

become pro. Are you a major leaguer? You can't run with the big dogs if you pee like a puppy.

This gives anyone who knows and listens to Dave Pratt insight that they should buy our books.

We have also received this *celebrity* endorsement from **Kevin Harrington, the original shark on the ABC hit television show *Shark Tank*:**

What I love about Yuloff Creative is that they become an in-house agency (marketing department) for small business owners. I think that's a brilliant idea. They think as if they are the small business owner's partner . . . . They are true mentors and coaches that are truly looking out for the best interests of their clients . . . . Over 30 years together, there's some wisdom going on here. You gotta check them out. Hank and Sharyn Yuloff, you guys are amazing. I'll see them in Sedona, you guys should make that contact right now too.

As you can see, this is a major "get" and you should always be on the look-out to develop celebrity friendships at any level so that if they get to know and enjoy your work, you may be fortunate enough to receive a celebrity endorsement.

We have received other celebrity endorsements for Yuloff Creative. Here are a few:

If you want to take your business to the next level, if you want to have a HR, and marketing department, around the corner, down the hall, across the street. These are the two you should work with. So, give them a call today or go to the website and have a conversation with them. You will be so grateful you did. **James Malinchak—ABC's *Secret Millionaire* and author of twenty books**

◆

Every business owner knows that getting help when you need it the most is important. And when it's important, Hank and Sharyn Yuloff are the business coaches to call. They are 'hand holders' and 'path showers' to get you over the hump and moving rapidly toward your goals. Get business coaching that builds your plan around you. Try their FreeMarketingConsulta-tion.com and see for yourself. **Joe Theismann— NFL MVP and Super Bowl winner**

Yuloff Creative helps entrepreneurs focus on one of the most vital parts of their business, marketing. It's true that sales drives every part of a business, but it's awesome marketing messages that turbo charge sales. [They] will inspire you to think more creatively, motivate you to take action, and help you improve your entire sales chain.

Larry Broughton—Founder & CEO broughtonHOTELS, frequent contributor to CNBC

Editorial Testimonials

Editorial third-party validation testimonials are difficult to receive and are absolute business building gold. This is getting a news publication or broadcast to talk about you in a positive manner. If you can get the *Wall Street Journal* to talk about you, your methods, how successful you are, or share what great work you are doing, this is going to assist your business. That "as seen on" or "as seen in" section is vital. When we are interviewed on networks or publications, or radio shows, we add those logos and links to our website.

Clinical Testimonials

A clinical third-party validation testimonial is the most difficult to receive. It is when you receive lab results proving your products are better. This is almost entirely for retail products, not services. This is why getting a testimonial from United Labs (UL) is important for all electrical products stating that the product you just bought is electronically certified as safe.

These testimonials are all good to have, and you must have them, but the further up the ladder you go, the harder they are to get. This brings us back to the scenario at the beginning of the chapter. The men who had the chance to post photos or talk about the fact that they had the opportunity to work on Air Force One, should have been screaming it in any possible way. Make the most of your opportunities. Let's go get 'em!

If you need assistance in learning how to get and third-party validation video testimonials, we suggest you grab a seat at one of our Small Business Breakthrough Bootcamps (TheMarketingEvent.com). We show you how to gather them and use them. You can also get us on the phone by signing up for a thirty-minute focus call where we can share some testimonial secrets with you. That is at www.FreeMarketingConsultation.com. We will talk to you soon.

7

The Top Ten Totally Necessary Parts of Your Sales Plan

"I have no idea where to start." It's hard to count the number of times that we have heard those words coming from business owners just like you. We all have a passion for our businesses. If you didn't, you would not have gone through all the effort that it took to get started. The fact is, most business owners were taught how to *do* what they do, but you were never taught how to *market* what you do.

Let's see if we can change that right here. In order to be as successful as you can be, you must have a plan to become successful marketing what you do. Here are the basics for getting to where you want to be.

1—Decide on your target market.
This is the most necessary part of your marketing plan. In our Small Business Breakthrough Bootcamps, we discuss how to decide on your target market. Quite often, we will have an attendee say, "Well, everyone could be a client of *ours.*" At that point, we pull up a slide that shows the top retailers in the recent past. We usually also show the 2014 chart which displays Amazon as being the first completely online company to break the top *ten* in the retail list.

The point being that as you look at the top ten or fifteen retail businesses, no one has ever said that they are a regular customer of all the stores, and rarely half of the top ten to fifteen. If most everyone cannot be a client of the top dozen retailers, why would *everyone* be a client of *yours.* It is completely probable that you will have more than one primary market and the demographics will be different for each of them.

2—Set your mission, goals and objectives.
Also, a totally necessary part of your marketing plan. When you have decided on your target market and ideal clients, you must then decide on your

21

mission, sales goals, and objectives. Your objectives could also be called your vision for the future—how and where you want to go. Your mission is how you expect to get there, and your sales goals are how fast you expect to be able to achieve them. When you are setting the mission, goals, and objectives for your business, be sure to factor in profit and beyond that, the way you would like to create your life.

3—Research your competition.
It is necessary to get a handle on your competitors. We have a new client that is opening a coffee shop and the main competitors are not necessarily a local Starbucks, an incoming Dunkin' Donuts, or McDonalds. They are national chains and we can position ourselves against them. Our real competitors are the local restaurants that serve breakfast and lunch that also serve coffee.

4—Create the right product.
Your marketing plan is to make certain that you are selling the correct product. There is an old saying that you should find out what your clients want, go get it, then sell it to them. This could mean that you adjust what you do for potential clients. For example:
- If you are a financial planner, you will have to focus on different products depending on the demographics of your clients.
- If you own a restaurant, it will depend on the type of food you are selling and the price point you want to achieve. It could also depend on the part of the country where you are located.
- If you own a promotional products company, you may decide on specific business niche or specific product category to focus upon.

Part of your creating the right product will depend on your exact clientele and what they need. It is entirely possible that you will have to change your product or parts of your product line.

5—What is your pricing?
Just the other day, I was at an event where six different people announced themselves as experts in the promotional products field. One of them, led with, "If you want the best and lowest prices, see me." How very disappointing. Just like fast food restaurants all feeling the need to have "value meals" which are low in price, but low in nutritional value as well. Always remember, you have the right to make a profit.

6—Create a message that is going to speak to your target.
These are the words that you are going to use. This is very important. Each of your target markets will be spoken to differently. Each of your target markets has a pain point—a level at which, when solved, will bring your product into the "buy zone." Take away their pain, and they will want to hire you.

7—Prepare a budget.
This is one of the most overlooked parts of a marketing plan by startup businesses and therefore the cause of their untimely demise. The budget keeps you from overspending on bright shiny objects that seem like a great idea at the time but were just a well-sold product. The rule of thumb for budgeting is that you should expect to receive a four to one return on your investment.

8—Create your website and social media platforms.
You need to create an online presence which will attract your target audiences and be attractive to them as well. Make certain your website is mobile friendly or you will lose all your search engine optimization. You should choose the social media platforms where your target audiences are spending their time and you should plan to touch them with communication every day. If you did not add a line item in your budget for a proper website construction, and proper social media preparation, head back and re-work that section.

9—Decide where to deliver your messages.
Now you need to take the messages you have created and place them wherever your potential clients are watching. Let's use an example. If your target market is small local businesses close to your business, then a local chamber of commerce is a great place to find them. If you are selling your product on a retail level, that may not be where you should go. You may want to be online or use direct mail. Don't be afraid to try a wide variety of message placement. This would give you a greater chance for success.

10—Evaluate your results.
Now it's time to do some fine tuning. Everything you do to market your business should be evaluated. We use a regular scale of A-F that you are familiar with from school. That grade level can be completely arbitrary, but consistent, depending on how you want to run your business. Here is an example: We have been members of many chambers of commerce. We decided to begin rating them and eliminating the ones which brought us the least amount of business or did not add us to their education schedules. We then took that

money budgeted for the underperforming chamber and directed it towards the others.

The same goes for each time you do a direct mail campaign, an email campaign, or a speaking presentation. Go over your numbers so you know in which directions to keep going or to stop.

Bonus—Change on the fly.

Don't you love to get more than you expect! Once you go over your numbers, or even *before* you come up with your numbers and see that something you are doing to market your business is not performing, do not hesitate to change directions as you go. It took us a while to figure out the right way to run our Small Business Breakthrough Bootcamps so they would deliver the desired results. This took lots of changes. Sometimes it is *during* the event, but regardless, we evaluate every bootcamp to see how we went.

If this helped you get on the right track or you want to get there, we are here for you. Simply go to www. FreeMarketingConsultation.com, fill in the short assessment and then grab a time in our calendar for a thirty-minute focus and breakthrough phone conversation.

8

What Are Your Ideal Clients' Demographics?

I had two conversations at one holiday party.
- Two people, both business owners, approximately the same age.
- Two *very* different attitudes about marketing.

The difference? Our first businessperson seems to have settled into a business with virtually no promotion and very little growth. The other? He's got *plans*! He wants an expansion of his business into a vertical one.

We were doing a Strategies for Success presentation for the Sedona Chamber of Commerce. So, let's use this as an example.

All the first person could talk about was that print ads don't work. Since I disagree, I gave some better ideas on how they could work, beginning, of course, with using the right print method and the right offer.

My tip? (Remember, we are trying to change someone's habits.) When a person sees an advertisement, they are deciding whether your company is worth trying compared to the current version of what they are using. As an example, if you had a favorite Italian restaurant, and it was a place that you had all your family events, how much of a deal would one of their competitors have to offer for you to change your habit and try the new place?

This person insisted that word of mouth was working just fine, thank you very much. Now word of mouth is great but saying that it is the *only* thing that is working seemed to ignore the fact that I am a client and I found this business through a networking group to which we both belonged.

As for the other business owner, he wants to expand his company vertically. All three of his current businesses and two new ones feed each other. With him, we discussed how to set up his entities (even got him a business lawyer referral on the spot) and we began to talk about a few online and offline strategies.

The point? Which of these two entrepreneurs do you think I see as a potential client for Sharyn and me? It's obvious, right?

It *became* obvious with the questions I asked each of them while we got to know each other. I *knew* the questions because I had my client avatars created in advance. *Both* fit the basic target: age, marital status, geography, income range, but for our business, there are some psychographics that go along with them. One of the most *vital*, is a measure of how excited they are about their own company—the more the better.

Manu Melwin Joy describes the demographic environment as:

- Age structure
- Gender
- Income distribution
- Family size
- Family life cycle
- Occupation
- Education
- Social class

What are the demographics and psychographics which determine the greatest possible success for both you and your prospects?

Do you know them?

Do you know the questions to ask that will "flip the switch" for both you and them?

Let's work on it.

Start by going to www.FreeMarketingConsultation.com and taking the short marketing assessment. Then book a thirty-minute evaluation (the site does it for you) and exploration call with me and Sharyn. We'll help you get on the right marketing path.

9

Human Resources Is Marketing and Sales

Lately, we have been receiving a lot of requests for career assistance. Some of those requests are coming through LinkedIn's Profinder.

While Hank spent his early years in sales, I began my career as a special education teacher helping severely emotionally disturbed children in a non-public school setting (K-12). Now, I now have over fifteen years in human resources. This means I can help you parlay your skills into a new role, too. I'll review and optimize your résumé, cover letter, and LinkedIn profile. I also provide mock phone interviews, so you are prepared. Lastly, I also help you identify and locate your ideal next employee and position you as their next ideal employee.

You *do* realize that all those collateral materials are marketing, right?

Your résumé is your marketing piece. As is your cover letter, your online presence (website, social media, including LinkedIn, etc.). And your phone interview. You are marketing yourself for your ideal next role. It may be only a target market of one: that specific human resource professional or the hiring manager, but it is marketing non-the-less.

The employer's job listing is their marketing piece. They, too, only have a target market of one: that one candidate who is positioned properly to show them that they are their next ideal employee.

Now I didn't always realize this. Before I joined Hank's business, I thought he was the marketing guy and I was office and human resource management. Then I was listening to him talk to his clients and realized that his conversations were the same conversations I was having in my small business human resources office.

This is probably an obvious point if you are freelancer or consultant, because you only get paid when someone contracts with you, but I postulate that it is also true if you are looking for a W2 role.

By the way, the marketing part doesn't end once your new employee is hired. Every day, employees and hiring managers have conversations that require one to convince the other of their position. I recommend that you switch your paradigm and think of these interactions with your marketing mind. How can you craft your message to attract your target market of one to your point of view?

If you would like help with your human resource marketing, whether you are a small business owner, a freelancer, consultant, or employee looking for your next role, please schedule a time with us at www.FreeHRconsultation. com.

10

Ways to Improve Your Sales Brochure

"Can you send us a brochure?"

Do you ever have a potential client say that? To me, they are doing one of two things. One, they are very interested but need a little more information before they decide to buy. Or, two, they are not at *all* interested and are just putting you off.

If it is number one, we need to make it so awesome that it reinforces their buying decision. But just in case it is number two, we need to make it so good that if they are in that category, they change their mind.

So how are we going to get that job done?

If you have been paying attention to the Yuloff Creative Marketing Solutions sales protocol, you know that our first brochure priority would be to write a book and begin to use that as your brochure. In fact, that might be the reason you are reading this book right now, we sent it to you after you asked for a brochure. If that's the case, how are we doing so far? Are you getting a good idea how we can help you and your business? You can do the same thing. And that's one way your client can say they hired you, "the gal (or guy) who wrote the book on the subject."

We'll talk about writing your book in the next chapter.

Did I just put a huge wall in front of you? Okay, let's back up just a bit and get your more traditional brochure done.

Here are ten tips to make it better than the average competitor going after the same business you are:

1. Promise me you will not use stock photos. Hire a professional photographer to get *great* shots of you, your team and the things that represent your company. The worst thing that could happen is that you use the same photos as your competitors. These photos *must* let clients say, "Oh, yeah, that's definitely me."

29

2. I learned a very cool rule for when it came to photos—the 20% rule. Make sure that the models in your photos are 20% younger, 20% better looking, and 20% better dressed than the people you are trying to attract. This is because that is how most people see themselves. For me, it would be a photo of Tom Hanks in *That Thing You Do*, George Clooney as Doug Ross in *ER*, or a taller Tom Cruise in *Top Gun*. Uh—better make that the 40% rule for me.

3. In addition to photos, pay a graphic artist to come up with a great graphic for the cover.

4. If you use digital printing (that means you can do a one-off instead of printing five hundred at a time and have them sit on a shelf for a year) you can personalize them for the person you are giving them to. Now, you might ask me, how do I do that with a book? Simple, I sign it!

5. Make sure you offer three possible problems that you solve and make yourself the answer to the challenge that the business is facing.

6. Along those lines, you can create a checklist to develop involvement by asking "How many of these benefits do you think will be included when you work with us?" Of course, you check *all* the boxes.

7. Each of our clients is different than their competitors. Our job is to help you focus on what those differences are and capitalize on them. For example, when companies work with Yuloff Creative, they get a team of experts. Most of our competitors are solopreneurs who cannot specialize on more than a couple of tactics. We easily double that number and together act as a multiplier. Point out what is different about your company.

8. You can also use a before/after comparison. Remember the Ad Council's "This is your brain; this is your brain on drugs" ads? A very powerful metaphor like that can improve success greatly.

9. Add an offer. Make it so good that they would have to be an idiot to not take you up on it.

10. You don't have to use an 8 ½ x 11 sheet of paper with two folds. There are *lots* of different shapes out there. Feel free to use them. By the way, that rule does not apply to business cards.

And, here's a bonus tip: Don't forget to test. See which offers work and then continue them. See which photos work the best. See which details work the best.

Obviously there are lots of other details which come into play, but these will get you down the road to success. Give us a call at 800-705-4265, or send us your layout to info@YuloffCreative .com, if you want help.

11

How to Write Your Book

Most of us for our first few books are still a bit intimidated with the entire process of creating a book. In past blogs we have talked about *why* to write your book, so now let's discuss *how* to get it done. I have broken it down into seventeen steps.

1. Put off the title. In the movies, you see the writing of a book portrayed all the time. The actor has a typewriter, puts paper in it and then . . . nothing. They are waiting for inspiration. That's because most people start with the title. Then, they think they must live up to it. Can you imagine naming your book *War and Peace*? And *then* starting out on Monday morning to write the book? We have gone through five titles for the HR marketing book—*The Marketing Checklist for Social Media Marketing: The Hows and Whys of Social Media.*

2. Instead, decide what you are going to write about. This is not hard—your industry! You are writing your book to be considered the expert. The literal "guy who wrote the book on the subject."

3. We got through steps one and two pretty fast, congratulations. Some of you are writing your book while you listen to or read this. Now create your chapter headings. Come up with about fifteen to *twenty* ideas of things you could write about under the topic of your book. Some people use post its on a cork board for this process so that later, they can move them around easily and see them all at once. Others use a white board. I write them down on paper. By the way, some chapters did not make the cut, which we will discuss later.

4. Now write one or two sentences on what is going to be in each chapter. Each chapter should be between one and *six* pages. That's roughly 150 to two thousand words. Another way to put that is one to three blog posts that you are combining.

5. Acquire an editor. Not your neighbor or your spouse. A real honest to goodness editor.

6. Decide on what research you may need to do. Set a calendar for getting that done within a fortnight. You should already know most of this stuff (it is not a doctoral dissertation). You might need a few statistics, if so, go get them.

7. Part of this research is to go through your blog posts and decide which ones will be included in your book. We have talked about this repeatedly; as you write your weekly blog posts, you are writing your book. You may have to edit them from informal to a bit more formal writing style, but that is partially what you have your editor for, to help you with that.

8. Once you have decided which blogs to include in the book, you need to write the rest of the chapters. Give me twenty-two minutes a day to write. Just before you check email. Each of your chapters are going to take a few days. This means your book is going to take about a month to write. If you have too many chapters or in other words are going too far over 100-150 pages, you may have *two* books. Don't put it all in one book! *The Marketing Checklist: 80 Simple Ways to Master Your Marketing*, really should have been "49 Simple Ways," to tie into *49 Stupid Things People do with Business Cards and How to Fix* them. Instead, *The Marketing Checklist 2* followed that theme with "49 More Simple ways." The marketing checklist books three, four, and five are being watched for content so that they can spill over into other books.

9. Go back and look at your chapter headings. Make them more interesting. You should be able to move to number ten which is . . .

10. Lock the title. And here is a tip which will make it worth the entire reading of this chapter (this includes the titles of your blogs): Use keywords someone would type to find you in the title.

11. Find someone to do your cover art. You can start this early in the process, but as you write the book, you may get ideas for what should go on the cover. Give your artist enough to read of the book that she has an idea of what to create for you. *Note*—and this is very important: If you are using your book to promote your business then you should be on the cover. This means that number twelve is . . .

12. Get great cover photos taken—by a professional. You can do this step at any time during this process.

13. Find people to review your book and give you a paragraph to put on the back of the book. Find the most well-known people you know. Hopefully, they will be people who have written books. While they are writing your reviews, you can move on to . . .
14. Have your book formatted and uploaded to the printer. I am not going to promote anyone, there are many.
15. This step is to take care of all the other stuff—the acknowledgements, the dedication, your author bio page, the copyright page, which your editor will assist you with.
16. Create the sales page—or pages. Keeping in mind that our books are sales tools, why not put sales pages inside them. It could be a coupon for your services. It could be how to get in touch with you to schedule an assessment appointment. Our books are getting more and more salesy. In the business card book, I thought I was being sly by adding a super-secret email address where people could have their cards approved. Now, we are adding full on "lights, camera, action" pages of our products.
17. Promote your book—but that is another subject.

12

Word of Mouth Sales Are the Best Sales— Ten Tips for Better Word of Mouth

"Word-of-mouth marketing is the only marketing I use." Uh huh. We hear it all the time. And it us usually followed by, "I get all my new business by word of mouth." Uh huh. And *that's* why you are at a *networking event* for the chamber of commerce every month!

Yes! We get it. Word of mouth *is* the best marketing. We get most of *our* referrals by word of mouth. But you must do *something* to create it. You didn't just open your business and people flocked to you, right? It's also the reason we grabbed the URL WordOfMarketing.com, because our response to that is, "We agree. Word of mouth *is* the best. And that's why we speed up your word of mouth by creating your word-of-mouth marketing program."

Here is one of my favorite stories about word-of-mouth marketing. I was at an Encino Chamber of Commerce lunch. At the beginning of the lunch, there is a round robin where each person at the table gets a chance to describe their business. I was the board of director's member at the table, so I had to go first. (Here is a random marketing tip: When you are in a situation where you are going around a table, sharing your story, try and take control of the table. Pick the person on your right to go first, and then say, "and you will go next," to the person on their right. This gives you the opportunity to hear what everyone else says and you can customize your presentation on the fly.) I shared my usual, "We are business coaches, specializing in improving your sales and profitability, eliminating your costly human resource night-mares, and putting you on your yellow-brick marketing path to the Wizard of Success." Sometimes I add that we own a promotional product company, or announce our next Small Business Breakthrough Bootcamp, or talk about our online do-it-yourself marketing plan that includes coaching—The Small Business Marketing Plan.

A new member, a contractor, said, "I don't need any marketing help, all my business is word of mouth."

"That's fantastic," I said. "Congratulations on your current and future success." As I continued, I noticed that he was wearing a t-shirt company with his company logo on it. When it was his turn, he passed around a brochure (with two typos, seriously), and a business card. I asked and he answered in the affirmative if the truck that he was to each of their jobs had a logo on it. He volunteered that they also put up a sign in the front lawn. He had also just spent $350 to join the chamber and $20 to attend the networking lunch. But *all* his marketing was word of mouth.

If you are noticing that so far half of this chapter is a rant, I am about to change that and answer the question, "How do I get more word-of-mouth marketing business, Hank?"

Thank you for asking! Here are *ten* tips to create word-of-mouth marketing:
1. Stay in touch with past clients. Often.
    - Text the following message randomly to clients: "I hope you are having a great day!"
    - Send birthday cards and half-birthday cards. Here is a great system that we sell. You can try for free at www.IDeserveItAll.com. They are real cards for less than $2 *including* postage.
    - Make random calls leaving the same "just wanted to say hello" message.
2. Use surveys to check out how you are doing. If you write them the right way, you can generate more positive answers, which generates more word of mouth.
3. Give your clients referrals! Nothing works better than sharing the love. This is one of the ways we show our clients that we want to get more word-of-mouth marketing by *giving out* the word-of-mouth marketing.
4. Allow your clients to blog on your website. We are updating our site and it will have a tab called "guest experts." What this is going to do for you is increase your website relevance, increase your backlink count with solid links, and gives you more reasons to promote your website that has nothing to do with your site. If you have a personal blog (nothing to do with your business) you could put it there, too.
5. Solicit, gather, and share client testimonials. In our Small Business Breakthrough Bootcamps, we discuss this a lot. They *must* be videos. Go to our web site to see an example of how simple they are.
6. Create a referral program. Here you are rewarding clients for assisting

in your word-of-mouth efforts. We like creating a points system for our client's customers that rewards them for various positive behaviors, like "liking" their social media site.

7. Here is the most basic reminder: Go above what is expected in your customer service, by making sure you have incredible staff and support.
8. Remember that *price* is not a big determinant of whether you get word-of-mouth marketing or not. If you offer a great product, the price, while important, is not the most important consideration.
9. Promote your clients on your social media and your blogs.
10. We have created a mastermind group of our clients. We get together a couple of times a year to share best practices. You can create a sense of community with your clients as well. The more you do this, the more they stick with you.

Bonus tip! Encourage reviews about your products. And, here are some statistics to back this up:
- 63% of visitors are more likely to buy when a website has reviews or ratings.
- Reviews can add 18% to your sales.
- Customer reviews are twelve times more trusted than descriptions from the company promoting its product.

One of the first slogans I used in our company is, "Marketing is everything you do when you are not doing what you do." All your marketing efforts are of course, designed to bring in new business, but make it easier by multiplying your word-of-mouth marketing efforts so that it makes it easier for new clients to find you.

Would you like help in creating a solid word-of-mouth marketing program? Here are two suggestions: First, come to our Small Business Breakthrough Bootcamp. We discuss a lot of different tactics in detail on how to create your word-of-mouth marketing program. Second, connect with us for a free marketing consultation. Head to www.FreeMarketingConsultation. com and you can grab a place in our calendar for a word-of-mouth marketing discussion.

13

A Sign of Things to Come—
Ten Rules for Your Outdoor Signs

Every brick and mortar business has the same challenge at the beginning—what is their outdoor sign going to look like? Let's go through a few rules to make your outdoor sign more attractive, and just as important, stake your place in the neighborhood. In fact, this signage issue plagues businesses that have been around for years. Let's look at your outdoor sign not only from a graphic design point of view, but as a sales generator.

Rule number one is that size matters. You should negotiate the largest sign possible with your landlord and your city. Always ask for a variance that will allow your outdoor sign to be bigger. If your landlord has more than one space open on the building's outdoor sign, you want the largest one.

Rule number two is that as large as your outdoor sign is, it will cost more to create and cost more to ship, but it is always worth it. See rule number one. One way to offset this cost will be to use lighter weight materials.

Rule number three is to remember that color affects the readability of your outdoor sign. There is a reason that stop signs are red and white. It's because those are the easiest colors on outdoor signs that the human eye can see. Yellow signs with black writing are the next easiest which is why that color combination is used for directional signs. You will have to take the color of your logo into consideration, but for words like "auto repair" or "dental office" or "car wash" which identify the type of business, not just the specific name of the company, you can get extra visibility.

Rule number four is that your outdoor sign is an invitation and a magnifier. Drivers need to be able to quickly see, understand, and react to your sign so readability is the top priority. It must be clearly seen from a distance. Rule of thumb? If your sign is at one end of a football field and the viewer is at the other, she should be able to read it.

Rule number five is to respect your weather conditions. The materials your outdoor sign is created with will likely have to endure a wide range of temperatures. This constant variance in hot and cold or extended periods of either can affect the lifetime of your sign. Make certain that the sign company has included this detail in the quote for your sign.

Rule number six is that Mother Nature has more than temperature to throw at your outdoor sign. Wind, rain, and snow can tear your company's sign from its mounting. Waterproof, solid materials are the best.

Rule number seven is to prepare for the security of your outdoor sign. We need to consider that graffiti is a possibility. Ask your sign company for a laminate that acts as a protective barrier and makes it easier to get rid of paint.

Rule number eight is to remember that a faded outdoor sign is harder to read. Father Time works with Mother Nature to allow sunshine to make your sign become harder to read. This can be offset by using UV inks that are resistant to the UV rays that the sun pounds down every day. We should *never* use water-based inks for our outdoor sign.

Rule number nine is that when the sun goes down, is your sign still able to be seen? Consider how your outdoor sign will be lit at night. Will it be lit from behind? Above? How bright can we make it? Brighter is better!

Rule number ten is that we want our outdoor sign to be legal. Prior to moving into a building, check with your local government for the rules that apply to signs in your area. Better to choose a different location than to be saddled with the inability to attract clients.

Bonus rule: When deciding what to put on your sign think of it as a business card that must be read and comprehended in four seconds. Here is a list, in order of importance, of what you can put on there, depending on the amount of room with which you have to work. We are using a client, 360 Automotive, located in Cottonwood, Arizona as an example.

- Your logo. If your logo is hard to read at a distance, then use clean, block letters.
- What you do (for example, 360 Automotive added "auto repair" over their logo).
- An important bonus. It could be that you are open twenty-four hours a day or that you deliver or that you offer free parking. 360 Automotive's is their warranty.
- Phone number.
- If you get co-op money from a supplier to help you pay for the outdoor sign, then their logo can be on there as well, but not to the detriment of your name and logo.

Another bonus rule: Make sure everything is spelled correctly. And don't put a QR code thirty-five feet in the air. We found an outdoor sign in Costa Rica that made us sad . . . and laugh.

If you want more information about how to create your outdoor sign, or signage of any kind, connect with us at www.freemarketingconsulation.com. We are your extra set of eyes to not only look at your outdoor sign, but your entire marketing program.

14

If your protest sign (or maybe your chapter title) needs punctuation, its message may be too long

We have all seen protesters holding signs on the internet that makes them look, frankly, dumb. We have also seen signs for a business on the internet that have bad punctuation and misspelled words. When we see them, what do we automatically think of the person who is holding that sign? Or that business? Yes, we think they are not all that intelligent. And we think less of them. If a prospect is considering giving you a check, would you rather she think you are intelligent, or not very smart? Of course, we all just choose intelligent.

So why let a simple mistake hurt your opportunity to increase your sales?

Most of the time the mistakes on signs are because someone rushed to finish them or neglected to proof them. It is easy for me to show you bad signs to get my point across, but what about mistakes in your presentations? Or emails? How do you think they make you look?

Take a few minutes to do what our elementary through high school teachers told us to do: Check your work before turning it in. It is sad how many people don't do this and by remembering this, you will add a few percentage points to your closing rate because your work will stand out from competitors who were too busy to pay attention. This is a small, incremental change you are making, but it makes all the difference in the world.

Let's talk about résumes, for a moment. When I was a sales manager for a national company, I saw résumes every week from people who wished to work for me. I knew I was not going to interview all of them. I only wanted to chat with the ones who met my standards. My first time through a stack of résumes was the "easy elimination round." That was where I took out all the ones with mistakes—spelling, grammar, and just bad writing style. Why? At that time, working for a promotional product company, misspelled words cost us money. If they blew it on their résume or cover letter, I could not take

41

the chance on them. Now imagine that it is one of your cover letters or emails with a proposal to do business with someone. Can you blame the prospect for not returning your call?

Why should they call you when you threw up a huge stop sign by using bad spelling, grammar, or punctuation?

To help you get over some easy hurdles, these are some punctuation rules to correct mistakes that we see frequently.

Period

We use them at the end of a declarative or imperative sentence.

> Our appointment lasted an hour.
> Bring back the rental car on time.

Use a period after initials, abbreviations, and contracted words.

N.F.L.	Mr.	*et al.*
W.W.F.	a.m.	oz.

Use only one period to complete a sentence which ends in an abbreviation.
Use a period, rather than a question mark, after an indirect question.

> He asked when we would be leaving.

Comma

Use a comma to separate words and phrases and in a series.

> Jennifer was not altogether happy, it appeared.
> Sam was frequently found studying, listening to music, and playing a game at the same time.

Semicolon

Use a semicolon to separate independent coordinate clauses closely connected in meaning when no coordinate conjunction (such as and, but, for, or, nor, or while) is used.

> Everyone's business did better after investing in The Small Business Marketing Plan; the average sales went up 47%.

Use a semicolon before a transitional word or phrase which joins the coordinate clauses of a compound sentence

> Jennifer was not excited about going to the baseball game; besides, the tickets were very expensive.

Use a semicolon in lists where a comma is insufficient to separate the items clearly.

Jennifer was deciding which features of The Small Business Marketing Plan she liked the most. She is choosing from the coaching feature; the fact that her non-profit gets a free copy; and that she gets to attend the live marketing bootcamps for free.

Colon

Use a colon before a list of items or details.

Jennifer bought The Small Business Marketing Plan because she needed help with three things: locking in her target market, closing sales, and using social media effectively.

Use a colon after the salutation of a business letter.

Dear Jennifer:

Question Mark

Use a question mark after each separate part of a sentence containing more than one question.

Should Jennifer give her free copy of The Small Business Marketing plan to the Boys and Girls Club? The Chamber of Commerce? YesICan.org?

Use a question mark at the end of a question.

What time yesterday did Jennifer buy The Small Business Marketing Plan?

Apostrophe

Use an apostrophe for contractions.

It's time for Jennifer to buy The Small Business Marketing Plan.

Or for the possessive case of a noun.

The Small Business Marketing Plan is now Jennifer's.

Exclamation Point

Use an exclamation point to express a strong feeling. You do not need more than one.

Jennifer is so excited that she bought The Small Business Marketing Plan!

Quotation Marks

Use quotation marks around a direct quotation. Do not use them for indirect statements.

"Wow," Jennifer said, "The Small Business Marketing plan is wonderful."

If you are about to have a sign made and want a second set of eyes to look at it, send it to Info @ Yuloff Creative.com. You can also give us a call at 800-705-4265.

15

How to Use Your Competitive Drive to Win

I know some of you are not baseball lovers, but if you get past the place where this story takes place, you will get to the meaning.

During a summer 2018 Boston Red Sox baseball game against the Baltimore Orioles, the announcers were talking about the fact that first-year Red Sox manager Alex Cora had told his team to be aggressive on three balls and no strike counts if the pitch looked good to them. That goes against the "unwritten" how-to-play-baseball rule that you make the pitcher work and take a 3-0 pitch because if he throws another ball, you get to take first base without the possibility of being put out. That led to a conversation about hitters who were great 3-0 hitters and commentator Dennis Eckersley mentioned two different players who took him deep (hit a home run against him) on that pitch, including Dwight Evans who hit a grand slam on that count. The other announcer said, "It still hurts, huh?"

"Yeah," was the response.

Later they were talking about the 1978 team that won ninety-nine games and how much it still hurt Eckersley that his team got beat in a one-game playoff.

"I think it might hurt some of them more than me, but . . ."

So why am I talking about baseball in a marketing and sales book? Competition. The joy of competition. The frustration of competition. The drive of competition. The winning in the competition.

One of the things that drives entrepreneurs, is that we want to be the best at what we do so much that the little losses and the big losses stick with us. It's the one at-bat where a guy hit a grand slam against a *hall of fame career* that *still* bothers Eckersley.

In another interview, Eckersley interviewed Kirk Gibson, who hit one of the most famous home runs of all time off him in the 1988 World Series.

Gibson, who got the better of Eckersley in that match up, later in the interview told Eckersley that he would have rather been in the Hall of Fame plus the championships that Eckersley had. Competition thirty years after the fact.

Do you know what drives you? What *really* drives you?

Another way to look at that question is, "do you know what your why is?"

We all need it. It's what keeps us going when we have that bad day. Or get that bad news. Or need to keep going to get a project done. Or write a blog that we don't really feel like writing. Or delivering some bad news to a client. I have heard it also called a "fire in your belly." To me, it is the thing that will always keep me moving forward to help our clients succeed. It is one of the things that we try and instill in them as well.

We suggest that you take some time and identify your why. Here are three examples of our whys:

Sharyn's why: I am a child-abuse survivor with a thriving business and a thriving (thirty year) relationship. I want to show other abuse survivors that they are not doomed to a life of misery; that they too can have a thriving business and relationships!

Hank's why: After witnessing a friend's family be blessed with an anonymous white envelope of cash during an unexpected funeral, I want to have enough funds to be the anonymous donor with a white envelope of cash when someone needs it.

Our mutual why: The middle class is shrinking. When we help enough small businesses grow large enough to hire one or two employees each, we will all be rebuilding the middle class (and our buying pool), regardless of government interventions.

Here is one way to create *your* why: What is it, the *why you do what you do*, that brings you closest to tears?

Are you looking for help in defeating your competitors? Developing your why? Taking that massive *why* you already have and getting it focused? Let's talk. Head to www.FreeMarketingConsultation.com, take the brief survey and grab a spot in our calendar. We will get you focused.

16

Ten Tips to Make Your Sales Surveys More Effective

Before we talk about the ten tips, a bit of history is necessary.

I receive dozens of emails every day. I am on a lot of lists and enjoy reading how some companies like to sell themselves. One of those lists is for an organization that I joined for one year. They work with an industry that puts on meetings and events. I had the promotional product part of our company join because I wanted to become a service provider of giveaways for their meetings. Most of the members of the group and therefore all their activities were located nowhere near our geographic home base. But I was willing to take a chance on the investment. The leadership of the organization, to a person, promised me that this would be a good move for my business, and that they would help.

It turned out to be a marketing fail. Their meetings were held at times that were inconvenient for me and at a distance which would have made it an average ninety-minute drive to get there. So, I did not renew and chalked it up to experience.

But I stayed on their email list . . . or rather, they *kept* me on their email list, and I continued to monitor what they did. Which brings me to our topic today: I received a survey email from the group.

Here is the email that came with it:

> Dear Hank,
> When you first connected with the XYZ Association you were promised insights and information that would help you overcome challenges and develop innovative ways to build your business.
>
> I want to make sure I keep that promise.

Before my quarterly meeting with the rest of the XYZ Association leadership team I want to find out what topics are the absolute most important to you. (*I interrupt here to say: this is not where the sales survey went. They did not ask about topics.*)

So, my question to you is this:
What is the single biggest challenge you're facing right now when it comes to landing new clients for your event planning business?
(Click here to tell me your single biggest challenge landing new clients.) (*I interrupt here again to say: Since the letter mentioned the "single biggest challenge" twice, this sales survey should have had three questions maximum.*)

If you could, please go ahead and do this right now—to make sure I get the results before the meeting.

A sales survey! I *love* surveys. How could I resist? I clicked the link and began the survey.

Question one asked me if I was in the industry or a service provider. I thought that this was going to split the survey two ways. But I was wrong. They were just asking. How disappointing because this meant that their information was going to be combined.

Here was question two: As a planner or service provider what's the single biggest challenge you face landing new clients right now? (Go beyond just saying "marketing." Please be as detailed as possible, the longer your answer the more value we can provide.)

They know that creatively promoting their business is the biggest challenge, but they are not certain how to assist their members, although they are an organization that supports those businesses. Here was my answer:

Well . . . as long as you asked . . . I joined your organization years ago. It was on the promise that the XYZ Association would help my business by creating connections with those who needed our promotional product services. Also, that some of the meetings were going to be more local to me. None of that happened in the year that I paid for. Over the past several years, we expanded our business to offer full marketing plans—taking small business owners down a marketing path which leads them to their prime, demographically correct clients. So, when I read this question, I think that most of them are not going to be *able* to give you a very detailed answer. Knowing what is "working now" in marketing is a very fluid challenge. Especially if you try and generalize to a large, diverse group. I think that to help your members, you need to help them drill down to who exactly is their target market. Once you have that, it is easier to "land" new clients.

By the way—the term *landing* is one approach—providing enough information which is helpful to your new client is another. Making yourself, your web presence, your collateral materials so incredible, that the potential client only thinks "of course" when it comes to the decision to hire you.

The rest of the sales survey—about twelve questions—was demographically filled, and I think that rather than waste the time of the member, they could have gotten the answers from the sign-up form when they joined:

- What is your area of expertise (What part of the industry do you work in)?
- How many events a year do you manage?
- What is their average budget?
- Do you have business insurance?
- Do you carry individual event insurance?

I say this because there was only one question which required the kind of answer which would get them some real data.

There was one very interesting question: What dollars have you invested in trade shows in the last five years? It seems an odd question, because it was the only question which asked about a specific marketing tactic. It made me wonder if the organization is planning to have their own tradeshow.

At the end I added my phone number and contact information. As of the writing of this book, I have yet to hear back after eighteen months.

Here are ten very important points to remember when putting together your sales surveys:

1. When asking survey questions, be certain that you are requesting information that will easily help you utilize the information to improve your service to those constituents.
2. When you are creating the questions, avoid organizational bias. This is an easy thing to happen and can skew the answers toward what you think the answer may be.
3. If necessary, or if you think you will get better, more complete

responses, explain why you are asking a question.

4. Create a mix of multiple choice and short, essay-type answers for your questions.
5. Make certain your introductory letter explaining the survey matches the questions.
6. Keep it as brief as possible—my rule of thumb is a maximum of ten. Tell your audience the number of questions and how brief a time it will take them: "This survey will only take five minutes to complete ten questions."
7. Thank them in advance for filling out the survey.
8. Thank them after they take your sales survey.
9. Offer them an incentive for filling out your sales survey. Everyone should get something, and a few should earn something more.
10. This is very important: If you are an organization sending the survey, you should tell them that the people who take the survey will receive a report on the data gained from the survey and what the organization is going to do with that information.

Bonus tip: This tip is a way to make your sales survey more effective by asking a bonus question. Ask your survey recipients if there is anything else they wish the organization to know. For example: "The board wants to keep its eye on the ball, and it's finger on the pulse of the industry. Is there anything going on in our industry or in your business that you wish to share with the board?"

Would you like help creating your sales survey or a survey that is going to be sent to your clients or employees? Call us at (800) 705-4265 and we will get started generating the kind of information you can truly use to improve your sales and marketing efforts. Please remember to hit the *subscribe button*.

17

Teaching Proper Phone Etiquette— How You Lost the Sale before You Had a Chance to Make It

We have all experienced *phone hell*. It happens when a business has not trained their receptionist, other employees, or the virtual assistant in the proper phone etiquette for that company. We enter phone hell when proper phone etiquette is not followed and one of a few things happen:

- The phone is *never* answered by a live person.
- The phone is answered by an answering machine and says, "Our options have changed," so, please listen to all of them before just pounding the *zero key* over and over so that you are transferred to an operator.
- The phone is answered by voice mail that is a machine voice.
- Once you are transferred to an operator, he speaks too loudly, too soft, too unintelligible, too fast for you to understand what he is saying.
- He transfers you to the wrong department.
- He hangs up before the transfer goes through, leaving you with a dial tone.
- He gives you wrong information.
- He tells you that he must see if the person you want to speak to is in, asks your name, then comes back and tells you that the person to whom you wish to speak is unavailable.

These are so many ways you can lose a sale, why make it harder on yourself by having your phone answered in an improper or unprofessional manner. There is really no reason for it, either. Let's assume that everyone we hire is in sales, no matter what their job function. Then let's train them that every time the phone rings, it is bringing sales into the company, no matter what the call is about. That means that raises, bonuses, and other benefits all go up when enough phone calls are handled using proper phone etiquette.

Let's look at the list above and see if we can solve some of the problems.

- Never answered. If there is no one to answer the phone, or you are a one-person company and are too busy to answer the phone, then hire a phone answering service.
- Options have changed. *No*, they have not. And if you are going to use this ruse to get them to listen to all the options, then do it in your voice, or an employee's voice. Use some different script, too. "Thanks for calling Yuloff Creative. We have several awesome options for you, and here they are . . ."
- Machine voice. When I get these, I think, "Are they still in business?" "Did I call the right number?" "Why are they so unprofessional?"
- The operator from hell. The person you hire to answer the phone *must* speak in a proper tone. Even if they answer the phone two hundred times a day, it must be stressed that the next call could be the most important call of the day. There is a joke that is used when someone makes a very silly error that goes, "You had *one job*." Yes, they have one job and I hate to say this, but someone must tell you. If they answer the phone poorly, they should not be working for you in that capacity.
- Transfers. They *must* be familiar with every department in the company. If you lose business because a call was transferred improperly, it is not the receptionist's fault. It is bad training. Create a chart called "Why People Call Us" or "Who Does What" so they can just look at the chart and direct the call properly.
- Premature hang-ups. Once again, the person at the front *must* be shown how to use the system.
- Wrong Information. "You know what, sir, I do not know who handles that at the company. I have been instructed that when that happens I am supposed to connect you with Mr. X because Mr. X knows everything in the company and will satisfy your needs. May I transfer you to him?" Then the receptionist must also follow up to get the correct answer.
- You're not in for that person? Have the receptionist be honest. If you are taking calls, take calls. If you are not taking calls, take *no* calls. Tell the receptionist that you have instructed him that you are in back to back meetings but will be checking for messages at the top of every hour and returning calls. Then return them.

The easiest way to make certain that the phone is answered with proper phone etiquette is to use a *script*. Tell your employees that "this is the exact manner in which to answer the phone." Let them know that they will be secret shopped to make sure that they are doing it correctly. When hiring for the receptionist position, part of your interview should be to have them mock answer the phone.

Have them create a list of questions that may not have come up during training so that you can both learn together. My first job was working at Thrifty Drug Store in Los Angeles. I was one of those who had to answer the phone and figured out that most of the phone calls that came in after 5 p.m. (we were open until 10 p.m.) were asking what time we were open until so they could get to the pharmacy to pick up their meds or the liquor department on their way home. I began answering the phone with, "Thank you for calling Thrifty Drug Store, Encino, we're open until 10 p.m. this evening. How may I help you?" Most of the time, the response I received was, "Wow, thank you so very much." Click. My manager heard me, noticed how little time I was on the phone, and it became store policy to begin answering the customer's question before they even had to ask it.

When hiring for the receptionist position, part of your interview should be to have them answer your calls. Give them a few tests. And for goodness sake, make sure you call their references for past jobs.

How may we help you improve phone etiquette at your company? Do you need to practice it with everyone on your staff? Do you need your virtual assistant to be secret shopped? Head to www.FreeMarketingConsulation. com. Take the short assessment and then we can talk on the phone, using proper phone etiquette about your situation.

18

Three LinkedIn Sales Letters That Failed

We're going to assume that if you are reading our sales book, you are looking for ways to improve your sales. One of those improvements is to use social media to connect yourself with people you have not met in person. We would like to postulate that sales done correctly promotes your best side. It shows your best face to the world. Proper use of language is the key to this part of your marketing effort. We recently received three letters through LinkedIn which did not do the senders any favors toward making a positive impression. In fact, only one of them received a return email from us.

Between the two of us, in LinkedIn, we have about 10,000 connections and growing, roughly two thirds of whom we have not met. When we get a new request, we take a quick look at their profile and send them one of our standard responses. We use a couple of standard responses because, a) it is easy and, b) to just hit *yes* in response to the connection is not helping us begin to build a relationship with the connection.

Standard Response One

> Hi (*insert first name*)! Thank you for connecting with me on LinkedIn. I follow my Facebook pages more frequently so it may be a good idea for you to like my www.Facebook.com/Our-MarketingGuy page and friend me up at www.Facebook.com/hankyuloff. At the OMG page you will get a constant stream of marketing tips and on the Hank Yuloff page you will get a constant stream of . . . well . . . me. Friend me up and let me know what a good referral for you would be so I will recognize it when I see it!
>
> Thanks again,

Sharyn (or Hank)
(800) 705-4265
P.S. (*We leave this blank to share something which might resonate with them based on their profile.*)

Standard Response Two

Thanks so much for connecting with me.

I wanted to reach out to you to say "Howdy," and learn more about you.

I took a quick look at your profile and I would like to know more about you and your professional background. Since I do a lot of networking and referring business, are you open to a quick phone call or cup of coffee?

By the way, how is LinkedIn working for you in helping you grow your business? I'm very knowledgeable about that platform (and Facebook, too) and might have a few suggestions for you to improve your results after we talk.

Once again thanks for the connection. I hope to hear from you soon.

All the best,
Hank Yuloff

Notice how we are letting personality show through, while remaining professional; no typos or fractional sentences.

We want to use this chapter to share three letters we received through the LinkedIn email system. Each person had sent us a connection request and received our standard response.

Email One

Hi Hank,
Please keep (*company name*)'s services in mind for clients in 2015.
(*Company Name*) partners with small businesses to manage Human Resources, Benefits, Payroll, etc. and ensure compliance with California labor and employment laws.
Sender Name and Info

Email Two

Hello hank,

Thanks for reaching out to me. I'd be interested in setting up a call. I'm curious though, are you just looking too add a graphic designer to your professional network or are you just trying to sell me some advice. Because if that's the case (no offense) I'm not too interested.

Otherwise I'd be glad to share a few things about my profession and possibly hear a few things about yours. I'm highly fascinated with marketing and I'm sure you are too.

Sender first name only

Email Three

Hey Hank thanks for reaching out My professional background is actually mostly Customer service but slowing building a UX brand. I haven't really used linkedIn to network most because of lazyness but currently on a 30 day goal of providing as much as value as I can give to people and trying to figure out how to brand my message of real world usability.

I am currently following M.S, T.L. and A.M. among others podcast so maybe they can provide you some valuable knowledge.

You can call me almost any time (*Phone*)

Thank you,

Sender first and last name

Our lesson for today is that when you send written communication, it should be solid. It should be something your high school English teacher would grade at a B or above level. This is especially true when you are communicating with someone new.

Remember the saying, "You only get one chance to make a first impression." So, take the time to make a good impression.

Another way to look at it is this: When Sharyn was the HR director for four different companies in two different industries, she received résumes daily, most of them were unsolicited. Her job was to read the lines but learn to read between those lines to understand the real story behind the person who was sending the résumé. Using this secret skill was one of her favorite parts of the job. It's also one of the things she loves to do now for our private coaching clients. The less detective work she had to do, the easier it was for the submitter to get a return phone call and an interview. Assuming they were right for the job, that interview was going to have a much better outcome for both parties, the better the résumé was crafted.

When Hank was a sales manager for a promotional products company, he had to interview hundreds of people each year. In order to narrow it down from the thousands of résumes he received, he had a process of elimination. Experience was one way, but bad cover letters and typographic errors were reasons for immediate elimination. Your letters and written communication through social media are a résumé, which is asking for business or to be referred. Make them count.

When you want help creating a perfectly clear image on social media, give us a phone call at (800)705-4265.

19

Using Slang in Sales Is So Yesterday

We all have slang terms which get used quite often. Some of them you will want to use forever, but others become quite dated. Ann-Marie Alcántara is a millennial in her twenties who wrote an article for Popsugar.com that had me intrigued. According to her, these slang terms are out:

Raise the roof	It is definitely out while pumping your arms toward said roof showing how old you are. Or that you are waving your arms in the air like you just don't care?
Tight	For a long time, this has been used to describe something awesome though now it is being used too loosely. But it *is* ok to describe a close relationship.
Chill pill	Don't tell people to take one. It's no longer a prescription for getting people to relax and take it easy.
What's the Dilly-o? Coolio and *Fo shizzle* and *Fo sho*	Are you white? Are you a rapper? Are you seriously using these terms? I do have one friend, about twelve years younger than me who continues to use the term *coolio*.
Peace out	As a way of saying goodbye. When combined with making a peace sign and tapping to your chest now just means you are a decade past being cool.
Cool beans	Might as well use *bitchin*. I have another friend who uses this all the time. All I can think of is that I like my legumes hot.
Stoked	When I read this word on the list, I was struck with a

bit of melancholy. I miss this word. Wait—if I *am* past using it, it is *very* old.

Hecka and *hella*	Both are used to mean *really*. Unlike *stoked*, I was *hella* glad to see these on the list.
My bad	A sarcastic apology. Delivered in a sarcastic tone. In my opinion, this should go away with *Just sayin'*. Absolutely hate that term.
Crib	To invite anyone to see your residence. If it has nothing to do with where your newborn spends most of her days, it is just wrong.
Fly	Hello, Jennifer Lopez, *you* are fly, but the rest of us are not going to use this.

Those are words which have fallen out of favor. Do you want to get ahead of the slang terms curve? Want to know the slang that is coming up? Jessica Chassin gave us a list on www.PopSugar.com and I have to say, I could only figure out a couple of them. You will see them being propagated on Tumblr, YouTube, and Twitter. My guess is you would also see them on Snapchat videos, but they disappear too quickly.

Snatched	Use it to describe anything that looks really good or on point. Your makeup or your suit or perhaps your sales presentation can be snatched.
Sus	Short for suspect. It is internet-speak for shady or questionable. For example, many people think that most politicians are *sus*.
Boots	It appears to be a modifier for adjectives or verbs to add emphasis. If you are really hungry, you say, "You're hungry boots." So, the word is replacing *really*.
Sis	This is the new *bro*. Just replace it where you would put that word.
Hunty	This would be your best friend, or posse or, I guess, your hunting party. If you are hitting the bars you bring your *hunties* to find a new person to hook up with. Speaking of hooking up, texting someone and saying you want to

	"watch Netflix and chill," really means you want to get together and have sex.
Stan	The internet's term for being a fan. If you are a fan of Guns N Roses and want them to reunite, you stan GNR. If you are stanning someone, you are actively being a fan.
Extra	When you think someone is trying too hard, they are *extra*.
Goals	When something looks good; something you very much admire or want. "Your hair is goals."
AF	The AF is abbreviation for *As F**k*. "Cool AF."
OTP	Slang for One True Paring. My wife, Sharyn and I are OTP. Can also be a couple you are emotionally invested in. My OTP is Penny and Leonard in *Big Bang Theory*. If they break up I would be upset.
Ship	It is one of the most important terms on the internet you have not heard. It comes from the word relationship. You *ship* the two people you want to be together. Before Leonard and Penny got together, I *shipped* them.

Now that you have been educated on the slang terms that are out of fashion and those which your children are using and which you may, at some time find as part of your own lexicon, watch how you use them in your sales presentations so they do not make you look funny.

If you want help in writing any of your materials from websites, to books, to brochures, ring our digits at 800-705-4265 and we will connect.

20

How to Improve a Company Website

Every year, because of the free marketing consultations we offer at www.
FreeMarketingConsultation.com we evaluate several dozen business websites,
looking for clues on how to improve a company website. One of the latest
company websites we investigated, seemed to have many of the characteristics
that we see all the time and it occurred to us that we should share these with
all of you so that you, too, can learn how to improve a company website.

We would like to share with you ten of the tactics you can use to improve
your website. This is not the entire list we check when we are improving the
performance of your website, but it will get you started.

1. Your website should be coded using WordPress instead of one of
   the many inexpensive plug-and-done website tools. WordPress is
   a website designing program that is made with open source code.
   This means that it is open for use by anyone without paying for
   the program. Within WordPress, the basic bone of your website, the
   framework, is where each part of the website lives. There are free
   frames available by the hundreds and thousands more frames that
   cost some money. The correct frame to use depends on the design of
   your website. Here is an important tip. Make sure that your frame
   has been downloaded for use at least 10,000 times. This gives the
   designers incentive to keep the frame up to date and bug free. Finally,
   because WordPress is open source, the search engines give them more
   credit when ranking them. This is a major strategy when you want to
   improve a company website.
2. Make sure that your website is optimized for cellular device usage.
   The number of searches which are done using mobile technology,
   compared to a desktop computer or laptop is growing steadily, so if

you want to know one of most important things to do, getting set for mobile is how to improve your company website.

3. Put your phone number on the front page, in the upper right-hand corner. We have read studies that say upwards of 60% of people will look at your website just to get your phone number, so let's make it easy. Also, when your target audience is looking at your website, your phone number should be "clickable" for easy calling.

4. Your social media logos, and therefore links should be on your site, and you should move them from the top of the page, where most designers put them, to the bottom of the home page. You have spent a lot of time and money to get people on to your website, let's keep them there.

5. You need to limit or eliminate the use of stock photos on your website. People could look at that photograph of the twelve professional people on your staff and wonder which of them you will assign to their case. When they find out none of those people exist in your world, there is dissonance. Dissonance leads to doubt which leads to not buying from you.

6. Make sure that you check all the links on your site on a regular basis. We just checked the website of a woman who is an executive coach and found two links which led us to a "404 Page Not Found" message. This, once again, brings us back to a state of dissonance. If you can keep potential clients out of dissonance, you are taking steps towards learning how to improve your company website.

7. When we look at the source code in the back end of your website, one of the things we look for are key words which are very important. When someone is looking for you, they go to the Google machine and type in the terms they are looking for. As an example, when you look for us, you will type in business coach, or *excellent* business coach, or business coaches who are experts in small business or many other possibilities. When we work with our private coaching clients, we do searches for these key words and add them to the code.

8. Many people get charged thousands of dollars for these searches, but for our private coaching clients, we want to make certain that we have the correct terms for them.

9. One of the best places to put those key words are on the tab for each page on your website. Those tabs are found above the URL at the top of your page. Most designers will mark those tabs with your company name and the page name. You are better than that! You should

not have it say "Yuloff Creative—Blog" but, instead "Top Business Coaching Team in the U.S."

10. *Video.* Add lots of it. On our website, and on our radio show—*The Marketing Checklist* (www.TheMarketingChecklist.com)—we have often discussed the importance of creating, using, and promoting video for your business. There is a video on our YouTube page, as well which can teach you the basics. When we work with our private coaching clients, we create a list of all the videos that a business needs and think you should do the same. Begin with a short video that goes on the front page of your web site, welcoming people *to* your site. It should be short, less than a minute, and professionally created. If you are looking to learn how to improve your company website, use video as a major advance.

11. The language you use is very important. You should look to use language that speaks to your target market instead of using newspaper style which speaks of you in the third person.

If you would like help turning your website from a basic pamphlet that does not assist you in sales, into a major tool in the sales process, do what many others do, and head to www.FreeMarketingConsulation.com, take the short assessment, and enter a time in our calendar for us to speak with you. We guarantee that we will find things that you can do immediately to improve your marketing in general and we can discuss how to improve your company website.

You can also call us at 800-705-4265, visit us at YuloffCreative.com, and join us for our Small Business Breakthrough Bootcamps.

21

The Point

"What is the *point?*"

I notice that when I am speaking in front of a group of business owners, I use that term a lot. Small groups or large, they all want to know the answer to that question.

Here's the point.

I tell a story, I bring it to the conclusion, and then I share the point. And that point is the message that the listener needs to hear and put into action so that they are more successful.

What is your *point?*

What are the most important things a customer gets from you?

Do you have the list? Have you tested that list with lots of clients and potential clients in order to find out which points resonate with the most people? Think about it then create the list.

And, when you're doing a sales presentation, get to the point quickly.

22

The Value You Bring

I recently learned something very important about presentations, and it was a personal lesson.

We held our Los Angeles edition of the marketing bootcamp and for the first time, I actually practiced most of my presentation. We had (for the third time in three bootcamps) completely changed most of the schedule and content. I was so excited to share what we were teaching, that I *had* to make certain that the message got across. The ROI for our attendees *had* to be palpable. And it worked. The connection that it made with our audience was far better.

It was different. As an event-oholic, I go to a couple dozen events each year and compare them to ours. I regularly observe that when other marketing people are on stage they seem them say over and over and over as part of their presentation, "When I work with clients, we teach them to . . . ." And most of the time, it sounds like a sales pitch. I have heard that often, even coming out of my own mouth. I realized that the difference between our Los Angeles presentation and most of the others is that when Sharyn and I are presenting we proceed to share good information after that statement.

The other day I sat in on another marketing person's event. In the first hour, he used that phrase five times and each time it sounded like he was saying, "You are only here to hire me. This event is designed to get you to hire me."

The take-away for this chapter is a simple one—when you are presenting, whether it is from stage, or in a one-on-one sales call—you need to offer solid value to your listeners.

Do *not* tell them that they only get the good stuff when they hire you. This is a digital age where people can get an answer on the internet and *even if that answer is wrong*, they can get it. Give them the good stuff.

23

Nine Bad Sales Habits to Break

Highly successful salespeople have developed some stellar habits. They didn't become one of their organization's top reps by good luck. They have honed their craft and become the best at what they do. On the flip side, many sales reps struggle to develop winning habits. Or, maybe they remain stuck in old practices that no longer generate sales. Whatever the case may be, it's important that you connect with prospective customers the right way and provide real value in order to close the most deals. It pays to take a step back and reflect on sales habits that might be harming your success.

Marketing and social media professional James Meincke has identified nine bad sales habits that hinder a salesperson's ability to close deals.

1. *Trying to sell to everyone.* Don't make as many calls as possible and hope that you land a few clients. That's not effective. Meincke asserts that it's much better to target your sales pitches to companies that are a good fit for what you're selling.

2. *Sending generic e-mails.* Considering that most people receive close to a hundred business-related e-mails each day, it's no secret that e-mail overload is a staggering problem. When you send a sales e-mail that is clearly from a template, you make it all too easy for the recipient to click "delete." Instead, aim to personalize your e-mails to increase your chances of getting a response.

3. *Calling without conducting any research first.* Don't waste your prospect's time by asking questions that can easily be researched. Before you dial their number, research the company and contact person. Use this information to inform your approach. By asking customized questions, you position yourself as a consultative partner.

4. *Still using B.A.N.T.* For nearly six decades, B.A.N.T. (budget,

authority, need and time) has been used as a tool to qualify prospects. However, the problem remains that this technique focuses on the seller's needs. When using B.A.N.T., sales reps are essentially asking questions to determine if the prospect is worth their time. Don't continue using this old-school approach. Meincke says the sales process—including qualification—should always be customer-focused. Make sure you put the customer's needs before your own.

5. *Overly stating someone's name.* You may think it's a good thing to keep saying a prospect's name to prove you know the person. However, it ends up coming off as cheesy and could potentially cost you the sale.

6. *Pretending you know everything.* Prospects know when you're making up an answer. It's best to admit when you don't know the answer to a question and commit to getting back to the prospect as soon as possible.

7. *Sending a follow-up e-mail simply to ask for a status update.* Nobody likes getting those "just checking in" e-mails. Every time you reach out to your clients and prospects, you should be adding value. Give them a link to a great article or provide an interesting piece of research. Never just "check in."

8. *Giving up on a deal too soon.* Sales, especially large ones, take time. Expect to talk to multiple people and complete many processes before closing a deal. Remain persistent and the effort you invest will eventually pay off.

9. *Asking prospects to print and sign a PDF.* Don't expect customers to shoulder all the work of printing, signing and scanning the documents you need. Invest in a tool that allows contracts to be signed digitally.

Are you guilty of one (or a few) of these bad sales habits? If so, commit to building better sales habits one at a time. None of us got into these bad habits overnight, so it could take some real effort to get out of them.

Your progression as a salesperson will not be perfected overnight. The better you are, the more you will continue to learn. When you stop learning, you stop earning!

24

Is It Time for You to Use Out-of-the-Box Sales Ideas? (The Answer May Surprise You)

I must tell you that the first time I heard that phrase in terms of sales, I thought it was a very cool metaphor for helping our clients become very different. It gives those of us who want to be fresh and capture our audience with our creativity an easy mental visual for what we are proposing to do.

But that is not where the phrase *out of the box* first came from. Originally, it was a way that information technology and software companies said that the software would work as soon as it was out of the box. In other words, there was nothing customized about the product for each user. It worked the same for everyone who used it. It was another way of saying it was *off the shelf.*

This is interesting to us because we have said for a very long time that the sales and marketing paths we create for our private coaching clients are anything *but* an off-the-shelf product. This is because we used to create a plan, in writing, and deliver it to our clients with a two-hour review period. We would then schedule a follow up in six months only to find that they had not taken if off the shelf. It had *stayed* in the box. Clearly that was *not* the way to generate success for our clients so we evolved our business model, or we began to think out of the box (wink, wink) and began to create a custom marketing *path* for each client, and work with them *in* their businesses on a constant basis to achieve the objectives we work with them to create.

When the word *think* was placed at the front of out of the box, it came to signify a new creativity. But then, it was used by so very many marketing folk that the phrase got overused to the point that it became a very off-the-shelf term for creativity.

It has gone right back to the beginning.

Let me share another thought about *think out of the box.* Sometimes, the box is very comfortable. Sometimes the box *works.* A century ago, having a book of business ads printed on yellow paper was a very out-of-the-box marketing tactic. Promotional products were and still can be an out-of-the-box marketing tactic, depending on the type of product and the way they carry your message. Having a website used to be a very think-out-of-the-box marketing tactic. Then social media became a very think-out-of-the-box marketing tactic. Coming up fast, you are right now hearing about artificial intelligence as a think-out-of-the-box marketing tactic.

Over time, all of those out-of-the-box marketing tactics became mainstream. In other words, *the box became a good and profitable place to be.* In fact, when we first sit down with you as a private business coaching client, we look at your box of marketing. We look at all the things that are *in* your box of marketing. We unpack your box full of marketing and see what is working and what is not working. Then we look at new and updated ways to use some of the ways we will market your business. In other words, we create a new, bigger, better, more creative box of marketing for you!

The tactic does not have to be out-of-the-box. There are dozens of marketing tactics that are very *in-the-box* normal, but when used in an unusual way or with a unique message, become *out-of-the-box* and cool.

25

Hitting the Jackpot
on Your Prize Wheel of Business Success

When we are hired by business owners to act as their business coach, we focus on their marketing, their sales, their human resources, and various other parts of how they run their business. We tell them that we want to be brought in on any decision they make that has to do with our areas of expertise. What they have done, by hiring us, is to spin the prize wheel where every slot is a winner.

One of our clients forgot to talk to us about a trade show, so of course, I must write about it. You see, I am an expert on trade shows, having exhibited at well into the triple digits and when you include the number of businesses clients that I have prepared for trade shows, it's up into four digits.

Our client was exhibiting at a trade show and used a prize wheel with eighteen different slots. That's a great thing, but they did not check with us before they put the prizes on that wheel. Here's what happened: They gave away gift cards that had nothing to do with bringing people back to their business. Instead, they gave away about five hundred dollars to *other* companies. That was a large percentage of what they invested for us to work together and we could have had them invest it more wisely.

What should they have done on their prize wheel? Thanks for asking.

We recently did a business expo for a local group of chambers of commerce. We used a prize wheel with that same eighteen slots. All the slots in this prize wheel brought people back to our business. Here is a list of what they said:
- Free marketing bootcamp (4 slots)
- Free e-book—*The Marketing Checklist 2* (3 slots)
- Free e-book —*The Marketing Checklist for Social Media Marketing* (4 slots)
- $1000 off private business coaching Program (2 slots)
- $100 off any promotional product order (3 slots)

- Wildcard (1 slot)
- The entire prize wheel (1 slot)

Here is how we delivered the prize wheel winners their prize:
- If someone won one book, we surprised them by sending *both* books. That's because we wanted to give them something they did not expect.
- If someone won a seat at The Small Business Breakthrough Bootcamp, we sent them a book, too. We told them that the book will give them a head start. We *also* told them that if they wanted an even bigger head start, they should sign up for a free marketing consultation and we will get them focused.
- If someone won a thousand off our private coaching program, we sent them a book, too. We also added the free marketing consultation.
- If someone won one hundred off promotional products, they got the book and marketing consultation link.
- If they won the entire wheel, we just sent *everything*, plus the consultation.

Why did we do this? Surely it was going to cost us a lot of money, right? That is not true.

The e-books have all been fixed costs that are long since paid.

The Small Business Breakthrough Bootcamp has fixed costs so adding a few more people does not cost us anything. In fact, it lowers our average cost per person attending.

The one thousand off our private coaching program *does* lower our profit, but when *you* refer someone who becomes a private coaching client, you get a referral fee and we have avoided advertising for that new client, so we are in effect recapturing that profit.

One hundred off a promotional product order makes that first order with us a zero profit, but we know that 75% of all promotional product clients who try us once, come back, so the long-term play is to give them that discount and have them become part of our tribe.

Compare the slots in our prize wheel to the slots of our client who forgot to check with us, and gave away coupons to coffee stores? His was a fixed hard cost that will never be absorbed and offset by other sales. The people spun, won a card, and went on their way. He could have offered to buy them coffee and solve their (his business) challenges over coffee.

When you are exhibiting at a trade show and are looking for cool ideas that will generate more revenue from your trade show investment, let's have a chat. Because whether it is a prize wheel, a drawing, or some other ideas to get trade show attendees to cross the invisible line and talk to you, we are here to advise you. For your free marketing consultation head to www.FreeMarketing Consultation.com and we will get you focused for your next trade show or everything else in your business. You are spinning the prize wheel when you go to FreeMarketingConsultation.com and you are a guaranteed winner.

26

Yelp and the Single Testimonials

I am amazed at how many businesspeople equate positive Yelp reviews with the best possible testimonials. As nice as it is to get someone to say, "I'm here because I saw your five (out of five) rating on Yelp," we have to understand that as a private company, Yelp is legally allowed to follow whatever rules of the road that the company wishes to create.

One of the heartening things about companies like Yelp or Trip Advisor is that consumers feel like they have a place to communicate via a third party with a vendor or store.

One of the disheartening things about companies like Yelp or Trip Advisor is that as a vendor or a store, you really have little or no control over what gets posted. But we still want those positive comments to be on the digital record.

And what we *want* to get is those testimonials on video so we can post them on our *own* websites and social media pages.

We collect testimonials because:
- Because everyone always says that *word of mouth* is the best marketing.
- Because *buying decisions* are swayed by testimonials—both positive and negative.
- Because if someone is searching for what we do, it would be a pretty awesome thing for them to find us because of a testimonial.

Let's talk a little bit about how to ask for testimonials. First, let's always be listening for a complement from one of our clients. Let's say you are a lawyer named Bob Epstein and you hear this: "Oh, Bob, you are the absolute best lawyer on the planet. I cannot believe you got fifty thousand out of that guy when he only owed me fifteen."

Bob's response should be: "*Thank you*! I appreciate your kind words. Say, may I ask you to put that testimonial on video for me, so I can help other people *just like you*? Just a few seconds will do it."

Some will. Some won't. 90% of the time it is because they do not like how they *think* they look on video.

Tell them you even have a card that will make it *super easy* for them to share their words (a security blanket to use during the testimonial in case they forget your name or what you do).

In the above comment, the phrase "just like you" is key. Psychologically, they will picture themselves, and you, and you helping others.

Important: As soon as they finish you say, "That was great! Can I get it just one more time, *just in case?*" The second one will always be better.

Here is what your card can look like:

YULOFF
Creative
**Marketing
SolutionS**

**I'm a Private Coaching Client with
HANK AND SHARYN YULOFF**
You should hire them because

They're completely invested in your success.

You'll have an in depth marketing plan.

They will ABSOLUTELY improve your business.

You'll Generate Immediate Results.

If you are too busy or not busy enough,
you should let them figure it all out for you.

My Name is: _____

Find Me at: www._____

We get asked all the time, "How many testimonials are enough?" The answer is the sky's the limit. More is always better. Video is better than written statements, but both are important.

If you want help creating and using testimonial videos, give us a call at 800-705-4265. And if we do a good job for you, please don't wait for us to ask!

27

How to Do a Year-End Sales Review

The end of a year—or a quarter or a month—is a great time for all those office housekeeping and year-end review activities. We recommend that you review the following areas that impact your sales and marketing program.

Marketing Report Card
This part of your year-end review will have you list everything you are doing to market your business and then give it a letter grade. You can be as subjective or as numbers based as you want. Here is an example of four things that we have done this year and how they were graded:

> *Sedona Referrals Club*　　　　B+
> Reason: We got enough promotional-product business
> to cover our costs and marketing-plan clients to make it
> profitable.
>
> *Encino Chamber of Commerce*　A
> Reason: Hank has remained on the board of directors and as
> our initial chamber it always has a warm place in our hearts.
> Hank was also awarded an honorary lifetime membership in
> 2017.
>
> *Teaching at OLLI* (Osher Lifelong Learning Institute) D
> Reason: Though it was fun, it generated zero business. It
> didn't even put us in front of a lot of people. This will not be
> repeated because though we were able to try out a few new
> teaching methods, that is not worth the time we invested.
>
> *Small Business Breakthrough Bootcamp*　　　　A
> Reason: This generated more business and leads than all

other marketing tools. We have six (maybe seven) bootcamps on the calendar for 2020. It gives us the best opportunity to educate the widest audience on how they must market their business.

The grade is arrived at from both a business objective perspective and a more subjective feeling. You should also grade each method based entirely on dollars generated. Are you placing ads in a local newspaper? Did you generate at least four times the dollars for each dollar spent? If not, give it a C. If it did, then a B or greater.

Review Your Supplier/Vendor Relationships and Contracts
This is an excellent opportunity to look at your relationships and agreements.
- Is your web hosting agreement up to date?
- Are all your agreements current?
- Is your credit card processor still giving you the rate they promised? Is their service worth the fees? What *are* all those fees?
- Are you satisfied with each supplier or vendor? You can create a list and grade them, too.
- Can you see opportunities for incremental growth by tweaking these relationships and agreements?
- Are there any areas that could even double your profit?

Emergency Planning
Climate change is teaching us all that we need plans in place to deal with weather issues. But your review is more than worrying about weather. Not everyone has to worry about hurricanes, but earthquakes, excess snow, and a truck running into a power pole can leave our business unable to function in our normal space. You need a printed binder of what-ifs that is copied to your entire management staff.

Think about it in terms of how disruption would affect your sales and marketing function.

Where will employees work and what is the protocol for checking in?

Are you able to access funds in an emergency?

Do you have backup sales materials in an off-site location?

There are a ton more questions we would ask here of clients, but you get the point. Walk through your office and ask a lot of, what-if-this-were-not-here questions.

We have a plan to run our entire Small Business Breakthrough Bootcamp without power. It would be more challenging, but we can do it.

Digital Assets Review

So much of what we do is online and electronic—we need to be sure that everything digital is checked on regularly.

Are your sales funnels operating? Do you need to change the offers? Do you need to A/B test them? Do you know what A/B testing is? (If not, you better call us.)

Is your website up to date? Does it still reflect your image? We just decided to change our name (don't do this twice in fifteen months without professional assistance) to Yuloff Creative Marketing Solutions so we need to phase out the Sedona Marketing moniker we put into place just two years ago. This meant that we had to change the SedonaMarketing.com landing page and video. We will update our main site next year, after fully launching The Small Business Marketing Plan, which, we decided in our year-end review, would take priority. What in your business needs priority attention?

Have you done a recent internet search of you and your brand? Are there any old phone numbers or addresses lurking on various websites?

Are your URLs about to expire? We caught three for two clients in one week which would have essentially put them out of business.

Is all the information on your business card up to date? I had to send a box of our marketing books to someone running a silent auction and the address on his card was wrong. When it came back (wasting forty dollars in shipping charges) he explained that he had changed it on his email signature but was just getting rid of the last few hundred business cards. His business is based on getting tiny details correct. I wonder what he misses in his business for clients. What if someone is sending him paperwork and has his card on their desk? What business is he losing?

Team Review

This part of your year-end review is not about who stays and who goes, but rather getting input from your team. Get them into the constant mode of asking for feedback from your clients.

I can always tell when a restaurant is not doing this when I ask a server if I can speak to the manager. More than 90% of the time they think they are about to hear something bad and when I tell the manager something wonderful about our experience, there is a reaction that indicates this is unusual.

You want your employees to be asking:

- How are we doing?
- What learning moments can we share with everyone?
- What are the three most important things we need to change in how we operate?
- How can we improve our training? Train your staff to be open to gathering information.

Before you have this open-feedback meeting, you should have your business secret-shopped. We call clients all the time to see how the phone is answered and how our questions are answered. That is the first line of contact, it should be strong.

You're probably thinking that your year-end review could easily be a year-long review. You are thinking correctly. The more we are open to improving, the more we are coachable, the better our business will be in the short and long term.

Would you like help putting your year-end review together? Have you done the review and need help with the what-now part of the process? Is now the time to hire a marketing coach and hugely improve your sales? Call us; 800-705-4265. Email us; info@YuloffCreative.com. Get in touch with us through social media. Or head to FreeMarketingConsultation.com and take the short assessment and then click the link to get into our calendar. We are here to help and look forward to serving you.

28

Targeting Your Audience with Each Sales Message You Create

"How do you speak to your target market?"

We hear that question all the time from our private coaching clients and entrepreneurs who attend our Small Business Breakthrough Bootcamps and who invest in our online program, The Small Business Marketing Plan.

Our overall answer begins this way. When you want to speak to your target market, you are planning to put the right message, in the right place, at the right time, so that when your target market is looking for you, your message is there waiting for them.

Let's talk about the right message. The most important thing to keep in mind when you speak to your target market is to remember that she is looking to solve *her* challenge, not ours. Approach your message from that point of view.

Here is an example: Cottonwood, Arizona is next to Sedona and like Sedona, derives much of its income from tourists visiting the area. One of the chamber of commerce executives, Karen Pfeifer, was asked to create a forty-five-second radio ad that would speak to locals, in the hope of developing local tourism dollars in addition to revenue from out-of-state visitors. She asked me to look over what she wrote and give some suggestions. Here is the original ad that Karen wrote.

> Hi, I am Karen, manager of the Cottonwood Chamber of Commerce Visitor Center. Come visit us at our new location at 849 Cove Parkway, in Cottonwood.
>
> We have maps for getting around our roads and for off road, and hiking. We also have information on our local attractions, Indian ruins, great restaurants, and wine tasting. Our old town area is a great place to sit and relax or do some shopping.

We are open 9:00-5:00 Monday through Friday and if we have a volunteer, available on Saturday and Sunday. Speaking of volunteers, we are taking applications for volunteers who want to join our team. Come in or call me 928 634-7593 and find out how you can become a volunteer.

All the facts are included, but what was missing was what was in it for the listener. Remember that when you speak to your target market, they might not be interested in hearing about you, but they sure as shootin' they want to hear about them and what you have that is in their best interest.

Here is what I wrote for the chamber. I began to speak to their target market, offering them reasons to stop by the chamber office.

Ever played tourist in your own back yard? The Cottonwood Chamber of Commerce will show you how to create your stay-cation with dozens of new places for you to visit.

Hi, I am Karen, manager of the Cottonwood Chamber Visitor Center. Come visit our new location at 849 Cove Parkway. We have maps for getting around our roads, and for off road and hiking. We also have info on our local attractions like Indian ruins and wine tasting.

We're open 9 to 5 Monday through Friday and if volunteers are available, on Saturday and Sunday, too. Speaking of volunteers, we're looking for vibrant volunteers to join our Cottonwood chamber team. Come in or call me at 928 634-7593 and find out how. That's 928-634-7593.

Your goal is to get the attention of the people who will most likely take the chamber up on its offer of free information. By beginning with a question, I capture the attention of all those who would answer, "*yes*." Those were the only people we were targeting.

So, remember this rule: When you want to speak to your target market, begin with what will capture their attention.

One last point: When you speak to your target market, you must remember that you probably have more than one primary target market, so prepare messages for each of them. Then you can place those messages, using the proper tactic, in the right place.

Would you like assistance with speaking to *your* target market? Connect with us at info@YuloffCreative.com.

Or, you can head to www.FreeMarketingConsultation.com. You will be shown a brief assessment, then placed right into our calendar for a thirty-minute review and planning session.

29

Networking for Those
Who Hate Networking

When we talk to new private business coaching clients about their first conversation with possible new clients at a networking meeting, we usually hear some variation of this, "I hate going to networking meetings. I always feel so . . ." followed by some word like "unsure," "alone," "detached," "unsettled." They even feel lonesome at a networking meeting.

We heard the other day from a new client. We were holding a full-day marketing planning meeting and when we came to discussing networking meetings, she and her partner who were financial planners both shared the same feelings. They are completely comfortable when they are in a one-on-one situation such as having a conversation with a potential new client, but when in a business crowd, at a networking event, they feel lost.

Thankfully, there was a chamber of commerce mixer that very evening, so we were able to witness their feelings first-hand, and do some things to solve their challenge.

This is not unusual. In fact, we hear some version of that story from most of our new business coaching clients. Many small business owners have the thought that they are new to the group and are not sure how to fit in.

We would like to help you get over those feelings if you often feel this way.

Even as business coaches, trained to interact with small business owners, we are not immune to these feelings. And as I write this, we are about to go into a brand-new networking meeting tomorrow morning. We just joined a new chamber of commerce in Arizona and have never attended any of their meetings.

Let's talk about the approach we are going to take—a different approach. When asked, most of our private business coaching clients have gone into the networking meeting looking for business. They want to find their target market and sell, sell, sell. They feel that if they don't find someone to buy, they have failed. We would rather set you up for success. How does that sound?

So, what is the plan?

Instead of selling *you*, we want you to put yourself in the position of a *buyer*. You are at the networking meeting hunting for new vendors.

You are also hunting for people who can connect with people you know. Being a connector is one of the best ways you can build your business. Here is a question you need to memorize: "If appropriate, what would I hear from someone that should make me think immediately of you?"

Did I promise to make connections? No. But if it is appropriate, you should start creating the contact list of people you can connect others with so they can decide if they are a match to connect with each other. And what are these two people who have nothing in common going to talk about? *You!*

Tomorrow, we will go into a networking meeting set up as a "speed dating" situation, where you sit across from another businessperson and for two minutes each, you talk about your businesses.

We will do it a bit differently. We tend to give them about three and a half minutes to "tell me your story in better depth."

No one else is going to do that.

What do *we* do with *our* thirty seconds? We do our regular elevator speech and then . . . and *then* . . . we give that person a copy of one of our best-selling business books. Sharyn gives out *The Marketing Checklist for Human Resources* and Hank gives out *The Marketing Checklist 2: 49 More Simple Ways to Master Your Marketing*.

Everyone else will be giving out an 8 ½ x 11 sheet of paper that sells, or just their business card. We give out a hundred-page book that assists them in building their business. Guess which one is more effective?

If you are familiar with The Small Business Marketing Plan online or The Small Business Breakthrough Bootcamp, you have been taught the power of books. This is where we bring them into play in a networking situation.

If you have not written your book yet, we suggest you create a tip sheet that you can give out instead of a sell sheet that talks about all the things you can sell them. Useful-and-needed defeats selling-like-mad every single time.

30

How to Make a Networking Meeting Work for You

Our first breakfast at the Greater Flagstaff Chamber of Commerce is in the books. It was a great experience! The drive from Sedona takes about forty-five minutes. In Los Angeles terms that is an average drive. What is not part of the LA experience is that there was light snow falling!

We arrived thirty minutes prior to the beginning of the networking event and since we were new, we made sure that we met the staff and the person who was running the event (Kat Ross, who is the vice president of investor relations for the chamber). It's always good to let the MC know who the new folks are. As it turns out, we were just two of twelve new attendees. I asked if they needed extra raffle prizes and handed her two copies of our book, *The Marketing Checklist for Social Media Marketing*.

We then took a walk around the perimeter of the room where the chamber had eight sponsors exhibiting. Each of these sponsors get a minute to speak to the room in addition to strutting their stuff at their tables. Each table offers a giveaway, which helps them build their list when each attendee drops their card in the box, hoping to win the prize. Note to self: The better the giveaway, the better the participation in the drawing.

The table-top networking took place in four rounds. You begin at table A and each person gets thirty seconds to share what they do and pass around their information. They then have a simple system that assigns where each person at the table goes next. Sharyn and I made sure we never ended up at the same table, and in the course of the twenty-five to twenty-eight people who each heard our elevator speech, we had about a third overlap.

Sharyn passed out our book, *The Marketing Checklist for Human Resources*, and I passed out *The Marketing Checklist 2*. Here is something very important that we noticed: *Most* often when people had an opportunity to get a book from each of us, they did not pay attention to the fact they were not getting the same book. In fact, a person who won our raffle prize, gave it to a friend, thinking that I had already given her that book. I emailed her an electronic version of the book that had been inadvertently given away. Marketing checklist tip: Always be free in giving away your books. They have *real* perceived value by the recipient.

We had joined the chamber prior to this networking event at the lowest membership level and were rewarded with the ability to put a flyer into the giveaway bag. Here is a marketing checklist tip that we will follow next time: Make whatever you put in the bag stand out. We put a free ticket to The Small Business Breakthrough Bootcamp into the bag, but I think next time we will put our flyer *into* or *attached to* a promotional product so that it stands out. Yes, that costs extra money, but standing out from the crowd is your main objective.

We met with Kat Ross afterwards and improved our membership to the next level which awards several benefits of putting us more visibly in front of the membership.

We also took a sponsorship of a table for the remaining three networking breakfasts of the year because we want to make a point of speaking to the group with the third-party validation of the chamber. Yes, you *pay* for that validation, but it is validation, nonetheless.

If you have been to The Small Business Breakthrough Bootcamp, you have heard us talk about the additional ways to put yourself ahead of the crowd. We are doing those things, too.

Do you want specific tips on how to market yourself to a chamber of commerce? Or in any networking situation? Sign up for a free thirty-minute breakthrough call when you head to www.FreeMarketingConsultation.com, and we will get you on the right track.

31

How to Boost Sales Success

One of the oldest sales rules is that when you wander into a prospect's office, the first thing you look for is something that you have in common. Is it a picture of the prospect fishing? Talk about the trips you used to take with your dad. Is it a picture of his kids? *Wow!* You get to chat with her about *your* kids. Let's move ahead a few decades from this premise and talk about representational systems. There are five of them and they are associated with our senses. Each of us favors one of them in how we learn and if you can master the technique of learning which one your clients and prospects favor, your communication with them will be more effective.

Here is how you can recognize the major representational systems.

Visual
People who are visual often stand or sit with their heads and/or bodies erect, with their eyes up. They often sit forward in their chair and tend to be organized, neat, well-groomed, and orderly. They memorize by seeing pictures and aren't often distracted by noise. They tend to have trouble remembering verbal instructions, as their minds tend to wander. A visual person will be interested in how your program *looks*. Here are expressions you can use to speak to them:
- How does that look?
- Looks good to me.
- I see what you mean.
- Let me paint you a picture.

Auditory
People who are auditory will quite often more their eyes sideways. They typically talk to themselves and can be easily distracted by noise. They can repeat

things back to you easily, they learn by listening, and they usually like music and talking on the phone. They memorize by steps, procedures, and sequences (sequentially). The auditory person likes to be told how they're doing and responds to a certain tone of voice or set of words. They will be interested in how your program sounds, and what you say about it. In addition to adding sound effects into your speech, here are expressions you can use to speak to them:

- I hear you.
- Sounds good.
- That rings true.
- It's music to my ears.
- That is loud and clear.

Kinesthetic

These folks tend to speak very . . . slowly. They respond to physical rewards and touching. They also stand closer to people than a visual person. They memorize by doing or walking through something. They will be interested in your program if it feels right or if you can give them something they can grasp. Get into your feelings and use these expressions to speak to them:

- Do you feel me?
- Reach your goals.
- Touch your goals.
- Results are within your grasp.

Auditory Digital

This person will spend a fair amount of time talking to themselves. They memorize by steps, procedures, and sequences. They will be interested in your program if it makes sense. These people can exhibit characteristics of the other representative systems.

You may be curious how to use these learning modalities in your work. While they are not a guarantee of closing the deal, you *will* help people capture your message. During our Small Business Marketing Bootcamps, we have coaching breaks after each section. To capture attention, we use sentences like: "In this last section, who saw something new?" And, "What rang the truest?" And, "How will it help you reach your goals?" And, "What this section means to you is . . ."

If you want help deciding which of the representative systems apply to you, connect with us and we will share a test with you that will demonstrate it. Call us at 800-705-4265 or go to FreeMarketingConsultation.com and you can get into our calendar after taking a short marketing assessment survey.

32

Why We Need to Give Back

"Hank and Sharyn," she said, "my business just got stable a couple of years ago. I think I need more time before I start to give back."

"I know we are pretty new," he said, "but we are determined to help our community."

Both business owners applied to come work with us at Yuloff Creative Marketing Solutions in order to get their business and their sales booming. They are both professionals with small staffs to support them and have been active in their communities for several years prior to opening their businesses. Based on these quotes, guess which of the two of these business owners we decided to work with.

It is a rather simple business decision, really. We preach that one of the ways a business is successful, is to know the demographics that they want to work with. For us, we have figured out that business owners who feel that their community is vital to their business, is one of the triggers which we relate to. And those business owners relate to us as well. Like relates to like. Here are some thoughts on giving back to your community and being involved:

- Politicians are involved with the community and you never know when having a relationship with your local politicians will be important to your business.
- It creates relationships with people who have the same mindset as you. We have worked with several companies we met when doing non-profit work that we and the owners of those companies believed in. We have also *hired* businesspeople we have met while doing work for the nonprofits which are important to us.
- You meet people to hire who believe in the bigger good. These are

the kind of people who stick around, especially when they see their boss is doing good work.

- It could increase your sales. There is a study by Edelman Insights Brandshare (2014) that says that people who feel a company is doing good things for society will purchase from them more often and recommend them to others more often.
- According to the Edelman Good Purpose study (2015) if your business is trying to be innovative, people will trust and partner with you more. That trust in you equals loyalty to your product.
- This one is really a bit self-serving, okay? When you are involved with a non-profit, and you are with them for a long period of time, they tend to want to thank you by giving you awards. Awards lead to positive press, which leads to more business.
- Sharpen your skills. By working with non-profits, you can develop skills. At their activities you will be called on to do things and learn things which you may not have done in your own business.
- We have heard lots of discussions recently from politicians talking about different *isms*. Without taking sides or putting forward any of my own feelings, just know that our society is held together by rules which include using our tax monies for the common good. If you are, like me, thankful to live in a society where our business is helped by these things (roads being built so our clients can get to us, fire and police departments to keep us safe, water and power departments which keep our computers running) then giving back is a logical step.

So, there it is, business owners, for the benefit of your business and to feel very good about yourselves, be involved with the community.

33

How Our Cats Increase Your Sales

When a speaker is in front of the room, don't you just love it when they begin by asking you to raise your hands?

- How many people love *their* cats?
- How many people are just *okay* with cats?
- How many people prefer dogs?
- How many of you really just want to get into the box of goodies over here?

We have three cats—one of which I love because he is just like a dog and shows unconditional love (Wally), another thinks I am okay as long as my wife is not around (Fenway), and the third treats me like her servant (Sweet Caroline).

What's the point of this? Let's say that your clients are like my cats—we can put them in the *sales triangle* below.

BUYING PHASES of
YOUR TARGET MARKET

Ready to purchase	3%
Open to Buying, But Not Looking	7%
They Aren't Thinking About You (indifferent)	30%
They Think They Aren't Interested in You	30%
They Know They Aren't Interested in You	30%

Source - The Ultimate Sales Machine - Chet Holmes

Now, I know, if you are not a cat person, I will probably lose you here, so pretend that I'm talking about having three *dogs*, okay?

So back to our cats. Wally represents the 3% ready-to-purchase clients. He has heard everything we have to offer, he has sniffed at our shoes and decided that we are a match for what he needs (especially that scratching all over stuff). And even when he is not in the mood to get scratched behind the ear, he is open to the idea of buying—the next 7% on this pyramid.

Fenway, who is really my wife Sharyn's cat, is one of those cats who could take or leave me. The only time she even comes near me is if Sharyn is not around. It does not matter how well I could scratch her behind the ears, she does not even think about me. In fact, if we are walking toward each other, she will go *way* out of her way to get away from me. This makes her the 60% of the pyramid that has very little interest.

Caroline, on the other hand, has so little interest in either of us, it's like having a stray cat living in our house that spends most of her time under the bed. She *knows* she is definitely not interested in having us scratch behind her ears or anywhere *else*.

There are a lot of sales trainers who would say I should only spend my time with Wally. They think that by giving any attention, or trying to give attention to Fenway or Caroline, I am wasting my time. They would think that by ignoring two of my cats I am spending my cat-time in the best possible place. That's because Fenway is barely, if at all interested, and Caroline is a lost cause. In other words, the rest of the cat market is ignoring me and what I can do for them.

We are believers in being able to niche down your markets, but I have always thought what happens if you focus strictly on one niche and that niche goes south?

The answer is you must have a back-up.

For the businesses we create marketing paths, we focus on small companies which are usually led by a couple (defined only as two people) who have had a good amount of success, but need help getting focused to achieve new levels of sales. But it does not mean that we avoid doing work for larger companies that need an outside set of eyes to look over what their internal team has proposed.

For companies that are in that middle 60%, you must have a program that will talk to them. With Fenway, I find that if I sit down at my desk, and pull another desk chair near to me, she will, sometimes, jump up on that chair and let me pet her. She won't do it when she is on the floor. But for that small period when she is up a bit higher, she will let my message of "I can scratch your ears really well" get through.

If I create a specific message for audiences who would normally shut me out, there is a chance that they will become open to buying from me.

As for that bottom 30%, Caroline, I must go to extreme measures to get her to pay attention to me. I must stretch my hands waaaaay under the bed, with chicken, for her to get near me. She knows she has zero interest even if I am giving it away. These are the clients who you can offer yourself to for free but they still don't get it. What is interesting is that a lot of our clients think they can get Caroline out from under the bed and spend part of their time with us in Sedona, trying to coax that cat out instead of working with us to create their marketing path to attract more Wallys and Fenways.

The point here is that I am supposed to keep feeding Wally, build a relationship with Fenway to make her as friendly as Wally, and put out enough loving vibes that maybe Caroline will come around. It's the same with potential clients. Keep feeding your Wallys, showing lots of appreciation and good will, but keep building relationships with your Fenways, who can become your Wally. It is how you can expand your niche markets.

As for Caroline, I will have to continue to educate her on my cat-scratch expertise, while not expecting to get her into my lap. I may be good, but there is 30% of my target market I will only sell if I have unlimited funds, or in her case, broiled chicken, and even then, she might not come out to play.

34

Keep Alert with Google Alerts

The internet is an amazing tool for sales. There are not many things that we cannot learn, nor share, using this tool. But how in the heck can you keep up with it all? And how do you find everything you need to know? And how do you figure out what is going on in your industry? And your competitors, how do you find out what they are doing? And Is what is being said about you positively or negatively?

There is a free tool called Google Alerts which can help you. By entering the search terms which are important to you, Google will help you keep track of the pieces of information which are important to you. It is as if Google is an employee, a brilliant employee with a fast set of fingers who is looking out for you.

One of our favorite ways to use this tool is to keep track of people in two categories—competitors and people we want as customers.

Now, before we get too far down the road, I want to just add the caveat that you cannot always believe everything you read online. You need to check your sources and make certain they are correct. That said, here is how to create an alert (taken from the Google page):

Sign into your Gmail account (if you do not have one, you can still use alerts). Go to Google Alerts at https://www.google.com/alerts#.

1. In the "Create an alert about" box, enter the words you want to get email notifications for, one term at a time. We suggest setting up different alerts for each of the following: your name, your company name, your top competitors, influencers in your industry, your top customers, and your top prospects. And, to get a little personal, we also suggest you set up the same for your spouse's name and your kids' names.

2. Click "Show options" to say how often you get alerts, what types of results you want to get, and more. Don't worry, you can always come back and edit your preferences later, as needed.
3. Click "Create Alert."
4. Once your alert is set up, you'll start getting emails any time Google finds new search results for your keywords.
5. You can also create an alert by clicking the + next to any of the suggested topics on the Google Alerts page.

Depending on the number of search terms you add to the alerts, you may want to decide how often you want to receive alerts. The internet is a very big thing! There could be a lot of alerts coming your way. You can also choose immediate notification for some things and once-a-week notification for things which are less important. You may want to set up a separate Gmail address for just the alerts.

I know some of you expect Google to be perfect. They're not. We receive lots of emails for the alerts we've set up that don't tell us what we were hoping we'd learn. It takes time to tell Google when you get an email that is not pertinent so that it learns. Sometimes it means refining the alert we've set up.

There are other tools that compete with Google Alerts that you may want to try (we haven't). Social Mention seems to be popular.

The key is what we do with that information. How do we react when someone mentions us or our work? Best advice, whether it is positive or negative is to take a breath, then another, and decide, "What is the best way for me to react so that my clients and potential clients will see me in a positive light."

Remember to stay on your marketing path and move ahead. If you want some help preparing for Google Alerts or other situations which may arise, go to www.FreeMarketingConsultation.com and take our marketing assessment. Along with that you get a follow up call with us to help you blaze that marketing path.

35

Do Your Own Sales Seminars

I get asked all the time how and why I began to put on my own seminars. I thought I would share the kinds of seminars we put on.

So, why put on our own seminars? Great question!

Speaking on stages is one of the best ways to establish yourself within your industry as an expert and to create an incredible sales funnel.

But when we are a beginner, sometimes we have a hard time getting onto other people's stages. So how do we get that valuable practice time?

Put on your *own* seminars!

When you put on your own seminars you get to choose the theme and have complete control over all the details. Of course, you *oversee* all the details and make sure that they all come together well.

We run three different types of events: short, medium, and long.

The short events are ninety minutes long. We call them Monthly Marketing Mornings. We run them in connection with business organizations, usually a chamber of commerce, though recently we did one for a United Way branch that puts on events for other non-profits as a way of developing community. These events are always free to the attendees, with one exception. We run several Meetup groups (MeetUp.com) which we tie into the Monthly Marketing Mornings and we charge a nominal $5 to attend. This money goes to the sponsoring organization (this fee pays for coffee and cookies).

The second kind of events we run are half-day long. These are free or very inexpensive in cost and for these, we partner with organizations as well.

Both short events and half day events give us valuable third-party validation as the experts in the group. When there is not a sponsoring organization, we have a minimal charge to cover costs.

The purpose of the first two types of events are to get people to a different event—our own several day-long events.

We run one- to three-day events which are inexpensive to moderately expensive as an introduction to our services. These are our own events sponsored by our company. The purpose of these events are to sell our products.

Many people use the longer events to sell *lots* of other people's products too, but that is not what we do. We prefer to offer a product of superior value, and not make it a three-day sales pitch. Our thought is that when we are on stage for upwards of *twenty* hours, it makes the eventual sale easier.

So far, that has proven to be true.

If you want help putting together your own events, get in contact with us and we will answer your questions.

After more than thirty years as a targeted marketing tactician helping small businesses get bigger, we might have some ideas to help yours grow. When developing marketing plans for entrepreneurs, we use creative ways to promote your brand and improve client retention while increasing sales and profitability. Go to www.YuloffCreative.com or call us at 800-705-4265.

36

Your Video Checklists—Basic and Advanced

For years now, in our Small Business Breakthrough Bootcamps and in far more detail, in our private coaching sessions, we have been talking a lot about the power of video from both the point of making your message known to your target audience and clients as well as giving the search engines something to focus on.

Now, we're going to concentrate in on making a better quality video for your clients and target audience. How you *tag* the video will make the most difference for your SEO.

The most important rule is to remember that you are shooting for your audience, not yourself, and not for someone else's audience—yours. This will make a big difference in your content—what you say in the video—because let's face it, you are using the video to sell yourself. When we put together marketing plans for clients who visit us in Sedona, we spend a lot of time working on this.

Here is your *basic* sales video checklist:
- Have the proper light.
- Make sure the sound is easily heard.
- Shooting outside? Distractions abound, mitigate them.
- Have an offer or a call to action.
- What is the point of the video?
- Announce yourself, twice—beginning and end.
- Is it timeless? Are you mentioning dates?
- Shoot often.
- Practice. It will make you better. You will get more accustomed to how you look and sound.
- Experiment—different angles, framing, the length of the video, how you speak.

- Be on the lookout for different ways to tell your story. Re-shoot it if you find another way to tell the same story.
- Don't be afraid to use a tripod. Or a lavalier microphone.
- Sometimes you will have to shoot it twice.

Understand that your audience is asking these questions: "What am I watching? What is this about? Why did that person just do that? Should I keep watching?"

Become very familiar, completely familiar with the equipment. Before I go out for a video shoot (ok, usually just before I go on vacation and want to make sure I get the right shot), I will sometimes review the camera's owner manual in case I find myself in unusual lighting conditions. But the more you shoot with your camera, the more your fingers develop muscle memory about the location for the control buttons. It will make for better video. By going through the manual, I sometimes find things I had not previously known, or had forgotten.

Here is your *more advanced* video checklist for your better sales videos:
- Step away from your project and come back to it the next day. Does it need any changes once a little time has passed?
- Watch the project without sound. Does the project mostly make sense? Is it entertaining and interesting?
- Close your eyes and listen to the project without visuals. Is it mostly understandable, entertaining, and interesting?
- Play each transition separately. Does the transition work? Would it be better as a straight cut? Are there any unexpected frames or sounds? Do any transitions need adjustment?
- Disable music and play the project. Is the project still good without music? Music should enhance the project, not come to its rescue.
- If there is text on the screen, is there plenty of time to read it aloud slowly? (In other words, does the text stay on the screen long enough?)
- Is there anything you can cut? Does every shot serve a purpose?
- Does your video answer the questions: who, what, when, where, and why?
- Is there enough visual variety? Variety can help keep a viewer's interest.
- Is there anything you could add to make it better, to improve the message, or improve the visuals? Sound effects, visual effects, titles, music, and voice-overs are tools you could consider for this.
- Is there anything you could remove to make the video better? (A

recurring theme in this checklist is to cut, cut, cut.)

- Do you have permission for everything you're using in the project? Music, photos, graphics, and people are especially troublesome areas.
- Is there any terminology (including acronyms) that won't be clear to the audience?
- Does the opening shot make a strong first impression? The opening shot is important. Did you choose a good one?
- Does the closing shot leave a lasting impression?
- Can your video be shortened to make it better?
- Would your audience (and possibly a total stranger) understand and enjoy this video?

37

Your Story—the Biography of a Sales Professional

When it comes to marketing yourself—telling *your* personal story and selling *you*, there is a positive and a negative outlook. The positive: There are ever expanding opportunities to tell your story. The negative side: There are so *many* possible places to tell that story, you are going to need many versions of it. Think of yourself as not just one person. You're an entire company—an entire baseball team of opportunities.

A quick note about first or third person, I think that third person is always best, but it is completely acceptable to have both versions available.

For this variety of opportunities, you are going to need a different line up of biographies that you can share with the different people who need them. Here are a few different bios to have at the ready.

The Lead-off Hitter—the Simple, Single Line of Text

Think of this as your personal slogan, your mission statement. I have heard other people say that this should be 140 characters or less (the Twitterverse effects everything, it seems). This is at the top of the order and serves as the basis of every other biography. You will use this bio as the introduction of your social media, the signature section of e-mails, and your business card. It could also be at the end of your blog sentence along with, "To connect with Hank, call 800-705-4265 or go to YuloffCreative.com."

> Hank Yuloff is a targeted marketing tactician, helping small businesses get bigger with creative technical and traditional marketing styles.

The Closer-in-the-Bullpen—Short Bio (50–60 Words)

This version is still going to leave them wanting more but builds on the brand message by giving up a few of the most essential facts about your professional self. Just like a closing pitcher in baseball, it gets the job done quickly and efficiently.

This biography is the one they will use in the program when you are one of many people at the event who are getting an award. Or on the chamber of commerce website when they want to share a little about each person. When you meet someone and they say, "What do you do?" and you don't want to be put in the same box as all your competitors, this is the biography you use. It should take no more than thirty seconds to read or speak.

If you are sponsoring a chamber of commerce lunch and they are introducing you to speak for five minutes, you can use this as your biography.

> Hank Yuloff is a targeted marketing tactician with more than thirty years' experience helping small businesses get bigger. He is the author of three best-selling marketing books and is a top tier producer in the promotional product industry.

> When developing marketing plans for entrepreneurs, Hank uses creative ways to promote their brand and improve client retention while increasing sales and profitability.

The Utility Player—Medium Bio (150–200 Words)

"We need a biography to put in the program."

I like this one, because they did not define what size to go with. Like a good utility player in baseball, it can be used in lots of places. Its longer form allows us to be more creative and add far more facts that will let someone know more about you and we can begin to tell our story. Relatively brief but informative, it hits all the important points of your story without sounding like it was written in bullet points.

This is a good size for a multiple-author piece and is the minimum size for your own website.

> Hank Yuloff is a targeted marketing tactician with over thirty years' experience keeping companies top of mind with their customers.

> er winning a contest to attend a Beatrice Foods stockholders meeting, Hank was given a Cross pen and pencil set with the corporate logo as a remembrance. Years later that meeting continues to shape his career.

> After graduating with a degree in advertising and public relations, Hank became a record sales leader for both a direct-mail

company and a promotional-products company before opening his own company in 1997, now called Yuloff Creative Marketing Solutions. They specialize in targeted marketing plans, client retention and appreciation, and promotional products. In 2015, they began offering two types of three and a half day events: For partner-owned small businesses, they create custom marketing plans in a focused, one-on-one setting *and* they host small group marketing bootcamps for demographically similar entrepreneurs.

In addition to authoring three books on marketing, Hank hosts a weekly radio show called *The Marketing Checklist*, with Sharyn, his wife of twenty-five years. They recently filmed an entrepreneurial mini-series with Brian Tracy called *Live Your List*.

And he still has that pen and pencil set!

The Ace Pitcher— Your Keynote Speaker Introduction and Long-Form Web Biography (300 Words)

When you are going on to a stage to speak, you have a prime chance to make a huge impression on many people. This is third party validation at its best. Like the ace pitcher in a baseball team's rotation, it is time for you to take the ball and perform in the big games. Since we are getting third party validation, this one *must* be written in third person format in two versions: the formal one, and the someone-is-going-to-be-reading-it one. The first is more formal, the second allows the person introducing you to sound human. This also means the second one should have shorter sentence structure so the speaker can take a breath.

When you are going to be introduced, they will ask for your bio in advance. *However, always bring a copy yourself* because there is a measurable percentage who will lose it. Print it out in *large copy* with difficult names spelled out phonetically (*ewe* loff).

The Clean Up Hitter—They Expect the Most (500 Plus Words)

This is the biography that goes on the personal website for you. It is going to be used when you market your book (on the back of the sales sheet). It is going to be used when you need to make the optimum impression. This is the one, like the clean-up hitter, that hits it out of the park. It includes *everything*. Your college degrees, main jobs, awards, noteworthy achievements, and things you have done to make the community a better place in which to live. You can even use it as the back-page biography of your books. I would suggest having a writer interview you and write it for you.

It is time to be the manager of your team and go make out your biography line-up.

As we end, there is a very important point I need to share; you *must* read and update these biographies on a regular basis. Things change in your life and in your company all the time, and your bio must keep pace. Here is an example: We filmed a mini-series, starring Brian Tracy, called *Live Your List*. The purpose of the series was to give some training to entrepreneurs and show them that even if they are busy, they need to remember why they opened their company and "live their bucket list." There are several teaching sessions in the series, and we were teaching the marketing session. In our bios, that went from the future tense, "We are very excited that in April of 2016 we are going to film this," to, "we just filmed this, and it is coming out soon." The series has not been released yet. That release date has been pushed at least two times. So, we have had to update our biographies to express those dates. When it finally does get released, we will have to update our biographies to talk about when and where it was available.

Do you need help with your biography? How about your marketing? If so, give us a call and we will make that happen.

38

A Modern Sales Story about a Modern TV Show

Several years ago, we noticed that the television show, now in syndication, *Modern Family* was doing a bit of product placement. A Toyota Prius was driven by Jesse Tyler Ferguson's character Mitchell Pritchett. And, Audi automobiles also got mentioned. Apple products have made many appearances including an entire episode shot on *i-everythings*.

This product placement was taken to an entire new level when the National Association of Realtors paid what we are betting was a huge fee to have actor Ty Burrell (Phil Dunphy) use an entire episode to explain in detail the difference between realtors and regular real estate agents. The N.A.R. also produced a series of ads starring Burrell that appear on other shows.

This made me think of another trend. During one commercial break while watching another show, I saw Burrell in the N.A.R. commercial, followed immediately by an Allstate ad featuring Adam DeVine (who plays Andy, Haley Dunphy's one true love) and *that* was immediately followed by an ad for Voya Financial starring Ferguson. It was a huge hint that *Modern Family* has taken over broadcast television.

We have seen Sofia Vergara (Gloria Pritchett) plug Head and Shoulders and CoverGirl while Julie Bowen (Claire Dunphy) has done ads for Neutrogena, Bridgestone Tires, and Olive Garden. Eric Stonestreet (Cameron Tucker) has appeared in ads for AT&T, ESPN, and Stand Up to Cancer. Sarah Hyland has been in Domino's Pizza ads and Jeep and Calgon.

Sharyn and I began to have a discussion on how the popularity of one product, in this case a television show called *Modern Family*, could impact the success of the products of another company. And that led us to talk about how our clients could get *their* products on a television show.

Do you want to get your products on to a show? Follow these rules and keep at it:

1. Make sure your product fits the character's lifestyle. It should blend, and not be noticed. If you watched a movie of *my* life, you would see a variety of brands (Dell, Toshiba, Sharp, GE, Canon, Sony, Apple, Toyota) all competing for attention, so I am willing to be bought!
2. Be able to easily explain how your product can make the show better. Will your Apple products make our home studio rock with better sound and video quality?
3. It is not going to be free. You are going to spend thousands of dollars per second unless you are the pet rock product of the moment.
4. Invite costume designers to press previews and showroom visits. Send them your product for consideration.
5. Tweet pictures to set designers, producers, and costume departments.
6. Make your pitch *directly to the point*. Be as brief as possible.
7. Be ready to sign the most one-sided contracts in your life including non-disclosures and pinky swears of secrecy.
8. Hopes high, expectations low. Producers turn down way north of 90% of requests. Only 2% of global advertising is from product placement.
9. Have a great story for why your product should be on the show. Have story ideas instead of press releases. Piggyback on timely news and current event marketing.
10. When you get on a show, use it to your every advantage. We have a client that does the picture framing for the stadium of a local sports team. Each time I see her do a thirty-second presentation, I have to remind her that she needs to tell *everyone*.

(Hey, since I am talking about it, we have noticed that the team of *Hawaii 5-0* has been driving Chevys and the bad guys *never* drive them. And as long as I am at it, *Hawaii 5-0* makes the state look like it is a haven for crime, rather than a perfect place to vacation.)

39

Bad Customer Service Almost Cost Celebrity Cruise Lines $100,000

The lifetime value of a customer is a number that helps companies focus their customer service activities. If you know how much that client is worth, you work harder.

Evidently, Celebrity Cruise Lines has not taught their bar managers that number.

Here is what happened on our recent cruise and then I will go over the numbers.

We were part of a group traveling in the Western Caribbean on the Celebrity *Reflection*. Sharyn and I were along as a continuing education program that was offered for marketing. Each evening, the group was meeting in one of the lounges, prior to dinner.

On the third night of the cruise, two of our party brought some cheese and bread into the lounge from one of the café's because they did not want to drink without eating something while they did. An hour or so after we were drinking (spending money as a captive audience), an officer of the ship who identified himself as the assistant beverage manager of the ship, saw the two plates, told us that food was not allowed in the bar, and had a busboy pick up the plates and take them away.

We asked why. He said that it was against the rules. Yeah, that did not make sense.

Where is it posted? It is not.

Where is that rule on the Celebrity.com website? Nowhere.

Where was it in the all the materials they leave in your cabin each night selling you *more* stuff? Can't find it.

I was incensed. Those of you who know me just can't believe that, right? I told the manager, why did you have to embarrass the two men who brought it down? Why did you not just ask us not to bring food to that lounge again?

Why did you waste the food? How are we supposed to know about these rules? What *other* rules exist that they don't tell us about?

And most importantly, *why are you treating us like six-year-olds when we just paid a combined $60,000 plus expenses to give you a job?*

I could not leave it there. I went down to guest relations and asked to speak with the hotel manager. I did not expect him to be in (but I don't know where he was going to go in the middle of the ocean) so I set a phone appointment time with him for the next morning.

He missed the appointment. And, did not call me or leave a message to let me *know* he was going to miss our appointment. Through his assistant, I set an *in-person* meeting at 6 p.m. for that evening in their office.

At 6 p.m., we showed up at the hotel manager's office. I was told he was finishing up another meeting and would join us momentarily. It *also* appeared that there were going to be several people in that meeting, one of whom was the beverage manager for the entire ship, Clint Kelu.

He asked if we would like to begin on time, and I said that would be great.

I laid out what had happened and when I told him that the service we received at that moment was more to be expected on one of their competitor's cruise lines (I used a specific reference), he seemed to flinch slightly. I asked the purpose of the bar rule. He answered that it was really put into effect because there are some foods which carry an odor which would not be in line with the theme of the bar. "But bread and cheese hardly seems like it would cause that unwanted effect," he said.

He apologized and explained that the officer in question had the option to not enforce that rule, and he should have let it go.

In fact, he was absolutely on board with our complaint and at no time did I feel he was just going through the motions.

He took the names of the other members of our party and said that they would absolutely receive an apology.

Taking the extra step, they also received a bottle of champagne.

Two nights later, we saw Mr. Kelu at a captain's reception. Not only did he instantly recognize us but apologized again and made certain that everyone had heard from him.

That is the mark of a company who sets a high bar and has the people in place to meet that standard.

So how about that lifetime-value number?

We are Captain's Club members of Celebrity. That means we have spent forty nights on their cruise ships. Including sister line Royal Caribbean, we have over forty nights on board their ships. And just two hours before the incident I am writing about, we had booked a nine-night cruise in Europe to celebrate our twenty-fifth anniversary. That's almost $8,000.

If you add another cruise at an average of $5000–$7000 per cruise every other year, in the next *twenty* years, we would spend $70,000 (not including money spent *on* the ship for shore excursions, alcohol, wi-fi packages, etc.) during that time period in addition to the over $30,000 we have spent in the past on that line (plus extras).

So, do you think that our cruise is going to stay on the Celebrity books?

What do your clients spend with you? Are you training all your people on that number?

If you would like help putting that number together or a training program for you and your staff, give us a call. 800-705-4265 We will help you keep business on your books where it belongs, and not let it sail away to one of your competitors.

40

It's Cheap to Be Affordable

I was at our networking group and as we went around the room talking about what we did I heard the same sorts of things:

- "I'm the best locksmith and we have cheap prices."
- "We work fast and cheap," said the painter.
- "And I am cheaper than the prevailing rates in Sedona," said the massage therapist.

I cringed each time I heard it—the word *cheap*.

I hate it when people devalue their product or service. When I think of all the training, effort, and time that they have put in to sharpen their skill sets, it saddens me to hear people compare themselves to the value menu at McDonalds.

This goes back a long way for me. I had a transmission-shop client who used to tell me that he didn't care if there was just enough ink in the pen to write the check to him, he wanted *cheap* pens.

I also remember doing the same thing *to* myself. When I began in the promotional product world, if someone asked for a polo shirt, I started by showing them the bottom-of-the-barrel shirts, thinking that I was going to solve their problem (they needed a shirt with a collar) in the least expensive (cheapest) way possible. What it took me awhile to learn was that when it came to the clothes people put on their staff and themselves, a certain level of quality, and therefore a higher price, was necessary. That was a huge hurdle for me.

Later, when it came to charge for marketing services, the same challenge confronted me. The first pricing structure we offered was very low. The idea was that an inexpensive add-on to our promotional product offerings would add an injection of cash to our profit level. But there was a mistake in this thinking. As you can see from the chart below, if you are a coach/advisor/ oracle, this is where you should be charging if you want to feel valued and, even more importantly, are *giving* incredible value for your services.

This information came from *Smart Meetings* magazine (April 2014):

Know the five levels of fee:

1. Unpaid: mediocre, starting out
2. $1,000–$2,500: get what you pay for
3. $2,500–$5,000: transition from part-time
4. $5,000–$10,000: hiring a true professional
5. $10,000+ bestseller or marquee name

In other words, if you *are* an expert, charge like an expert. The services we offer are commensurate for the value we add to our client's businesses and that makes what we do *affordable*.

Do not turn yourself into the lowest price alternative. You *cannot* make it up on volume. You are *not* the McDonald's value meal for what you do.

Now let's have two as-long-as-I-am-at-it moments. As long as I am at it, when I hear people use the phrase, "give me your best price" it shows me that they do not respect the skill and the benefits they get from working with the person they have just insulted. I had one person recently ask me for a referral to work with one of my team members rather than me. He said, "I'd like it to look professional without the professional price tag. Lol!" I connected him with my team member and added 20% to his rate. He's worth it. And so are you.

As long as I am at it, the terms we use make a big difference. What we put into our minds, makes a difference in what comes out. Here are several examples how are you using these words?

spend vs. invest
cheap vs. affordable
problems vs. challenge
complicated vs. detailed
I *have* to vs. I *get* to

Or to put it a more amusing way—one word can make all the difference in your business. How? Would you rather your child receive sexual *education* or sexual *instruction*?

Your words are powerful Watch how you are using them.

41

How to Create Your Facebook Live Broadcasts and Fourteen Types of Live Videos to Create

Since Facebook Live appeared on the scene, whenever we were on stage speaking to small and large groups about how to market their businesses, we would ask two questions: How many of you have *heard* of Facebook Live, and how many of you have *done* a Facebook Live broadcast?"

Within a year, we went from *zero* and *zero* to about 90% for each question. Clearly this is a marketing tool that is skyrocketing from obscurity to incredibly popular.

Quite often we would stop our marketing presentation and *do* a Facebook Live broadcast just to make sure everyone knew how to use this tool that is going to be as common on Facebook as uploading a photo or a plain text post.

Since this is going to be a here-as-long-as-Facebook-is tool, we want to share a simple system for having a more effective Facebook Live broadcast and generating more business by using them.:

1. Before you hit the "Go Live" button, write a brief description of what they are going to see in your Facebook Live video. We like humorous or catchy comments.

2. As soon as you press the "Start Live Video" button and you get the "Live" message, you should introduce yourself and your business. I figured this out when I had the epiphany that when your target audience shares your videos, the people who see you for the first time really should know who you are.

3. Just as you would at the beginning of your blog posts, tell your audience what you are going to be discussing in the Facebook Live video, and what they are going to learn.

4. Teach your content. It's why people are on your Facebook Live stream so deliver what you promised in the description at the beginning."

5. As you see people pop on to your Facebook Live stream, say, "hello," if it does not interfere too much with your teaching of content. We *want* engagement, so this lets them know you appreciate that they are watching and commenting.

6. Remind them who you are by giving them your name and website, then add in your *call to action*. You should always tell your audience what you need them to do next. It could be to subscribe, or *like* your business page or, to do something like we always do, send them to www.FreeMarketingConsultation.com to sign up for a thirty-minute free strategy call.

7. Save the video to your hard drive so you can use it in other places. You may want to use it as the video that rides along with your blog post on the same subject. Google the instructions on how to save it. We would share the instructions, but it keeps changing. Here is how we use the content. For example, we did a Facebook Live broadcast during our radio show, *The Marketing Checklist* (episode 228) where we discussed Facebook Live. Then we wrote a blog. And, that blog became this chapter.

Here are fourteen different content ideas that we have used and are now sharing with you.

1. Interview one of your clients and talk about them and their services. You are putting them on center stage on your page. We have interviewed several people that when you Google them, the first listing is our interview of them because of how we use key words in the description and tags.

2. Customer testimonials. When your customers come up to you and praise the work you are doing for them, pull out your phone, fire up the Facebook app and capture those positive words on video. Download it and share it to your website as well.

3. Give testimonials for people and companies who have done great things for you. Make certain you tag them, so they know you did it.

4. People love behind-the-scenes videos. We do them when we set up for a trade show, and the small business breakthrough bootcamps, and before a speaking event when we arrive early and are getting a feel for the room. We also do them when we are driving *to* an event. If you watch our Facebook personal and business pages, you will see us doing Facebook Live when we cross state lines on our way to a speaking event. It's our way of telling our local audiences—to quote

Todd Rundgren and Grand Funk Railroad—"that we're coming to your town, it's time to party down!"

5. Go live during one of your events. Quite often, when Sharyn is on stage, and leading the discussion, I will grab my phone, open the Facebook app, and go live while she is sharing social media or online marketing tips. It took a while, but she is getting used to it. And, you will too! These live-during-events broadcasts are the majority of what you will see on Facebook and can be the most fun. Remember to make sure that you have your introduction and closing scripts ready before you hit the "Go Live" button.

6. You can announce breaking news. When something really cool is about to happen, or just happened, like when we were selected to participate as finalists in the Marketing of the Year competition it was worth sharing on our pages. I also did a Facebook Live stream when I received a Lifetime Member Award from the Encino Chamber of Commerce.

7. You can create a regularly occurring show. This is the same thing as putting together a podcast. The biggest difference here is that you will have to be dressed appropriately. We have done segments of our radio show, *The Marketing Checklist*, on Facebook Live. It takes more work but is a lot of fun. *Very important*: If you are doing a regularly occurring show, make sure you are *regular*. Pick the time and be consistent.

8. A Live tour of your facility. If are having an open house at your location, give a tour while people are walking around. You will probably get a lot of testimonials that you can repurpose later. You don't have to be having an open house, you can have the tour and save it for your website.

9. Announce a new product. This is a great way to let the world know you have something new and exciting going on. You can build up the anticipation for weeks in advance, giving hints as to what is coming.

10. Explain and display that product—or any of your products. We have gone to promotional product trade shows and shot lots of product videos in one day. We then shared them for a *year* on our social media pages and through emails.

11. Announce a new event. Just like letting the world know you have a new product; you can let them know you are having an event. This is a Facebook Live version of save the date.

12. Tips on how to use your products. The biggest search on YouTube

is for *how-to* videos. You can use your Facebook Live videos to teach how to use your product or service or website.

13. Personal stories. People love to know the person behind the title. This is a great way to help them do that. It is also a great way to introduce new members of your team.

14. Offer content to a private group. Our private business coaching clients get access to a private Facebook group to get questions answered and to network. We also give them super-secret Ninja marketing tips created just for them.

As a final note, we want to share something very important. *Before* you do your Facebook Live video, you will want to announce that you are going to *do* a Facebook Live stream. It could be an hour, a day, and even a week before you go live. Remember that we are looking to generate engagement and if you have something special that you want to share, let your audience know in plenty of time so they can plan on attending.

You can *also* re-share your Facebook Live video after you have stopped broadcasting. By repurposing and reusing your brand-new digital asset, it makes the time you invested in creating your Facebook Live video more valuable.

Would you like help in knowing what to put on your Facebook Live broadcasts? Go to www.FreeMarketingConsultation.com and take the short, easy assessment. You will then be put right into our calendar to choose a time that works for us all. We would like to assist you.

42

Competition Gives a Small-Town Feeling in a Large Town

I never gave much thought to competition, and always just assumed that it existed and was a part of life. In every marketing tactic I have sold, newspaper—direct mail, promotional products and the like—competition was a constant.

But living most of the time now in a small town, I have gotten a very different view of competition and how it effects the marketplace. A little background is in order. Prior to living here, in Sedona, Arizona (population 10,000 or so), we lived in a suburb of Los Angeles for seventeen years. Prior to that we lived in *another* suburb next to it for *five* years.

In those time periods, we settled into both neighborhoods. We found *our* dry cleaner. We found *our* gas station. We found *our* store (you know, I wonder why we all call our grocery store just *the store*). We found *our* Mexican food restaurant and all of our other *ours* which turn the big city you live in into your small manageable neighborhood.

Some of those *ours* were locally owned. Getting great service there was not difficult because we always dealt with the owner. In fact, if there was anything wrong, the owner fixed it immediately. It's why we did not mind paying a little bit extra and having it take a little more time for an oil change at the locally-owned place compared to the drive-through chain.

Some of the *our* places were chains. But we figured out that by knowing the people running the stores, the service level was the same as if it were locally owned.

We turned the second largest city in the country into a small town.

Then we moved our base of operations to Sedona and had to find a whole lot of new *ours*. Logically, our first expectation was that in Sedona, it being a small town, every business would be run as if it were in a small town.

For the most part, boy were we right. Small retail business owners in this city are very eager to get the work from locals. In fact, many of the restaurants have a locals discount that we have found to be pretty awesome. So, though it is a small town, the amount of competition has made it advantageous to the stores to do a great job.

There are two types of businesses that were unexpectedly in need of our services—local chains and local services. Let's talk about each of them.

The local chains remarkably, do *not* have a small-town feel. In Los Angeles, we have used a chain bank for years and I wish they had a branch here. But alas, no. We decided to use another national chain with a presence in Arizona and . . . well, the service . . . is wanting! Same for the local national office-supply chain. They might as well be in the middle of L.A. because they act as if we will only be in their store that one time (somehow we find ourselves there about once each week).

But the most important thing that needs improvement is the mañana attitude of local tradespeople. We needed some things done around our office, so we had the opportunity to study about a dozen different trades. The one thread that runs through all of them (roofing, construction, drywall, blinds, locksmiths, window washers, and more) is their lack of commitment to *return a phone call*. We think that the lack of competition is what makes the small town uncompetitive to large towns. The pattern is the same with all of them. Here are some examples.

We saw a locksmith in the parking lot of a hardware store. He had done some work at our office and we are wanting more done. I handed him a card and said, "Whenever you have a day, an hour, or are just in the neighborhood, give us a call." His answer was that he'd get around to it. No call in three months.

We met a blinds vendor at a chamber of commerce mixer. I explained that we have several windows which need blinds and that she should call us so we can do some business. Still waiting after *six* months.

We needed drywall done. Six calls to three people to get someone to do the job.

A window washer who works at the west end of town thought we were too far away. A twelve-minute drive. He spends most of his time off-road riding his bike.

I have always thought that the saying attributed to Woody Allen that "80% of success is just showing up" was a bit too high. But I grew up in business in Los Angeles where competition is high, too. What I have now learned, from asking friends around the country, is that Woody may be on to something.

I make a lot of my blog posts into a checklist for success in marketing, aiming at between five and ten tips which will help you, my clients and potential clients, build your business. But today, I give you one tip.

1. Answer the darn phone and return a call.

If you want to become the *our* for all of your clients and minimize the competition, give us a phone call at 800-705-4265.

43

When It Rains, It Pours

When it rains, it pours.

We've all heard this expression. It means that when things go wrong, it can be like a domino effect. It starts out with one thing and it just keeps on going: You have a flat tire, then your battery dies, then your muffler falls off.

I'd like to use the expression to mean something else when we talk about sales and marketing messages, and the number of ways we market our companies.

When it begins to rain, we can see each individual drop as it hits the ground. As more rain falls, those drops begin to combine and cover the entire ground. When we moved our private business coaching company to Sedona, Arizona we noticed that when it snows, this example is more dramatic. If it is not cold enough, the snow does not stick. It melts on impact. But if a lot of snow falls in a small area, it stacks up and sticks around.

Let's use this as a sales and marketing analogy.

When you send out a few sales messages, using a small amount of tactics, your messages, like individual drops of snow, do not cover enough area to increase your sales. When you have many sales messages being sent out through many methods, far more people see your message and it would be more effective.

The question always gets asked, "Gee, Hank, so how many sales messages do I have to send out? How many ways of marketing my business do I need to use?"

That is an awesome question. And, since marketing is a science of choice, the answer is going to be—it depends. I know, not a very good answer, right?

Most every sales and marketing expert will say more is better. As a targeted-marketing tactician, my answer is to start with at least five and begin to chart the response you get with each tactic. The tactics we use when we put together your marketing plan are not random; they are the marketing messages which make the most sense. They are the sales and marketing messages which, when placed in the proper places will end up in front of the correct eyeballs.

Here is one warning on where you place your sales and marketing messages: Don't just do what your competition is doing. Don't just do what your friend who owns a different kind of business does.

44

Solicitations through Email

Every holiday season I am bombarded by a bevy of nonprofit solicitation emails. They have become sort of a hobby. When you are on the contact list for dozens *of* nonprofits, getting nonprofit solicitation emails in December comes with the territory.

The hobby part of nonprofit solicitation emails is to see how many of them are poorly executed. They expect you to just hand over the money because they are a nonprofit.

Another part of the hobby is to see which nonprofit solicitation emails are executed well. And my favorite nonprofit solicitation emails are the ones that with a few changes could be even more successful.

Most nonprofits are not as successful as they could be. Simply put, it is because they are not militant for their cause. They approach us with their hand out, palm up, and expect us to drop coins because they are a nonprofit. They fail to understand that the 501c-3 designation is just a tax status. They can make a profit. They *should* approach us, hand up, with a piece of parchment in hand, showing us what they do for the community. It should be a list of what would not be getting done by private business or government if their nonprofit did not exist.

A way for a nonprofit to understand the impact of their message would be to picture themselves as an observer of their actions as James Stewart did in *It's a Wonderful Life.* He saw with his own eyes what would happen if George Bailey did not exist. Another way to picture this is Ebenezer Scrooge gets to see with his own eyes how much different his life could be if he was more giving to the right places. These are examples of considering the impact of your actions on those around you—considering the user experience.

This lack of sales ability is why so many nonprofits struggle. It is also one of the reasons we offer a free copy of our product, The Small Business

Marketing Plan, to the nonprofit of choice to the business owner who invests in the program.

Here are three examples of what I received in the last week of the year. My ghosts of Christmas-nonprofit-solicitation-emails past.

First is from the Cancer Support Community. They sent it to me at 4:12 p.m. on New Year's Eve. They should have been making their case a long time prior to that. Their message is not a very strong one—no stories and no photos. The subject line of "Only a Few Hours Left . . ." does not reach out to me, either.

The next is from a local hospital. They had gotten to me earlier in the week and had been asking since Thanksgiving. Their subject line assumes I am finally thinking about tax deductions the last two days of the year. Their headline is missing a *why*. Or more specifically, a "Y." What if they had reminded me that I had just one more chance to support *my* community instead of *theirs*. They have a good photo, showing me their medical team in action, but I must read down into the body copy to find out that the money is to support their emergency department. This campaign brought in over $150,000 thanks to a very large matching donor. They did not even mention this in the email which is disappointing as it would increase donations. What is great, however, is that there are two direct phone numbers that allow you to speak to the nonprofit directly.

The last email was from Citizens for Responsibility and Ethics in Washington. They gave us a time limit, and a reason to donate in the subject line. That increases the likelihood that the email will be opened. They gave us compelling reasons to donate and how the money was going to be used. They also highlighted a matching donation which lets me see that I can donate an amount and it would be doubly effective. One more thing that is *great* about this email is that on their donate button, they are telling me that it is secure to add my credit card.

I have brought up tactics which can be used year-round to improve your nonprofit solicitation emails that are fundraising for your nonprofit. If you want more help, give us a call at 800-705-4265 or, even better, take our free marketing assessment at www.FreeMarketingConsultation.com.

45

A Marketing Fairy Tale

I'd like to tell you a marketing fairy tale.

Once upon a time, the incredibly popular band Geraniums N' Grenades released their fifth album and it sold ten million downloads in the first week. It happened again the next week and the next, causing their management to alter the plans for the Geraniums N' Grenades summer tour.

Instead of hitting sixty of the largest cities with averages of 15,000 people, they *lowered* the number of cities and *added* some shows in ten places where they could do shows of over 100,000, some as high as 200,000. These mega shows were going to be more profitable and make the image of the band begin to hit *legendary* status.

The marketing of these shows included some brand-new ideas. Since the name of a hit on the new album was "Knocking on Your Door," they wanted fans who lived in the same neighborhood to carpool to the mega-shows but needed a way to get them to know each other.

Then came *the idea*.

For $4, plus $3.95 shipping, fans going to the show could pop The Smirk on a Stick into their front yard and get other Geraniums N' Grenades fans to knock on their door and make arrangements to head to the shows together. The Smirk was based on the sixties happy-face image and was a six-inch circle which was attached to a three-foot stick in the ground.

Carpools meant having fewer cars which meant fewer parking spots used, which meant more booths to sell merchandise outside the venue. The kicker was that they got the tour sponsor, LearnToPark.com, to give everyone a $10 coupon when they turned in their Smirk at the concert. The LearnToPark. com logo and their URL were on the stick. Band management saw this as a win for the band because The Smirks cost them nothing since LearnToPark. com paid for them. The fans saw it as a win because they could show their appreciation for the band and make a profit on the deal. The sponsor, Learn-ToPark.com, saw it as a win, because their own market research showed that a $10 coupon increased the average sale by $30. Plus, the $2.00 they paid for The Smirks was given back to them by the band, who kept the other $2.

The band even promoted the green-conscious action of carpooling.

Excitement mounted, and so did the number of hours of entertainment news coverage for Geraniums N' Grenades, as videos of neighborhoods *filled* with Smirks on a Stick in front lawns showed up on screen. The concerts all sold out and Geraniums N' Grenades made five million dollars more than expected.

So, here is the question: Who got fired?

What? Fired?

This is a marketing situation which caused lots of problems for Geraniums N' Grenades. Though this is a made-up story, we think you have an idea of what happened. But the challenges were rather widespread. Incredible marketing ideas must be thought through, and every angle must be checked.

Here's what happened that caused all the problems.

During the Geraniums N' Grenades concert tour, there were 876 break-ins at the houses which displayed the Smirk on a Stick. If burglars were paying attention, and they were, you would be able to tell exactly who was going to be out of their homes and for what time period. Though there were fewer break-ins later in the tour because of publicity, Geraniums N' Grenades will feel the sting of this for years. In fact, they are going to have a difficult time using unusual marketing methods ever again.

So, who got fired?

The tour PR firm who came up with the idea. The band wanted to promote "Knocking on Your Door" and the firm went big but did not think it all through.

The band got fired by the sponsor, LearnToPark.com, who was tarnished by the break-ins. The sponsor received millions of dollars in backlash and bad publicity just for being part of the event. Since they saw a break-in as a form of abuse, they offset the challenge by creating a fund for www.YesICan.org which helps victims of abuse seek help.

And, the head of the band's security detail was let go because the band said, "he should have known." He is currently studying for his private investigator license.

And finally, the band created a fund in each of the ten mega-concert cities which paid for overtime for police investigators working the robbery division. This caused them to fire the lead singer's glorified babysitter who spent most of his time drunk in the hotel lobby. Actually, everyone in the band thought he should go and this gave them a great excuse to fire him, so there *was* at least one positive outcome.

Marketing is a science of choice, but it does not have definite mathematical axioms. We must look at the human aspects of what we are thinking of doing to promote our companies. We also must be flexible to make changes on the fly as new information becomes available and the situation changes. This current-events marketing, using the current atmosphere surrounding us, is an important part of our marketing plan, which must be consistently reviewed and updated.

Also, since it takes more than just sticking a sign in the ground to create great marketing, call us and we will help you establish a plan that will be music to your ears! (800) 705-4265.

46

How to Say *Thank You*
to Your Referral Partners

Most businesspeople and entrepreneurs rely on referral partners for a decent percent of their new business. At various times in my career, depending on how you are counting, (number of clients or dollars generated) that percentage has been as high as half, but usually clocks in at between 15– 20%. The relationships you develop with potential referral partners may be more important than knowing your new prospective clients. For example, after coaching sessions with us, Angie Lozano of Angie's House learned that in order to fill her affordable transitional-housing properties, she needed to spend more time speaking to her referral partners (parole officers and discharge planners) than speaking at twelve -step groups. We also have a business broker client that learned a better way to promote himself within networking groups in order to create better relationships with his referral partners.

When developing referral partner relationships, a lot of entrepreneurs are concerned that they do not have much business that they can send back as a referral. Even if the referral partners do not expect a quid pro quo, everyone would like to see more business come their way.

- Let's talk about some of the things you can do besides referring work to stay top of mind—and on the radar—of your referral partners.
- Make your referral partner look good by doing a good job. I know you *always* do a great job; I am just reinforcing that notion that we must all, always stay on top of our games. If your new client can tell the person who referred them that you are *amazing*, you will get more referrals, faster.
- Appreciation wins out over self-promotion. Remember when you got cash for the holidays from a relative and Mom told you that you had to send a thank-you note before you could spend it? Same thing applies. Send a handwritten thank-you note even before you are sure

you will be hired. We use our SendOutCards account and it's done in a breeze. (Try it free, on me if you wish—www.CardsByHank.com.) One of our clients recently told me that they have met other business coaches, but they want someone who appreciates their business. You may want to add recognition during the holidays as well by creating a list of referral partners who not only get your holiday card, but gifts as well.

- Keep the referral partners in the loop on the work you are doing. If the client relationship allows it, find out if and how referral partners would like to be kept informed about their clients' matters, especially if something may affect the work they are doing. We have had a web developer refer us to help his client create a marketing plan and write the copy on the website. I shared information as we went and reinforced the positive decision that our mutual client made in hiring that developer.

- Build that relationship. Take referral partners to lunch and ask about their companies. What kind of business are they seeking? Who is their ideal customer or client? My favorite question is to ask, "How will I recognize a good time to refer to you?" Let them know that, when appropriate, you will do your best to identify opportunities.

- Make introductions. Even if you don't have business to give, you have contacts to share. We were just able to refer a brand-new company that attended one of our Monthly Marketing Mornings at the Cottonwood Chamber of Commerce to an accountant in their new state. The connection was made by e-mail, but the first thing they have in common is us!

  We know a realtor named Karen Piet that holds a monthly informal breakfast mixer at a locally owned coffee shop in Flagstaff (Cedar House has incredible coffee.) for people she has met that she thinks need to know each other. And while we are talking about building relationships, the first time we went to Karen's mixer, because we were new to the group, I looked for someone in the crowd that I could give a testimonial for instead of just promoting us. There was a printer there—The Printing Raven—who had done some great work for us, so I was able to reinforce that relationship by thanking Tracie in public.

- Include them. We have invited our referral partners to our Small Business Breakthrough Bootcamps so we can easily connect them with others. Since we are on stage at the front of the room giving those referrals, they carry extra third- party validation and our referral partners feel even more special.

- Return the favor. If you can, send business back to people who are referring business to you. Obviously, this needs to be in the best interest of the client. Keeping track of your referrals both coming to you and the ones you make is a good idea. Follow up with both parties regularly.
- Be strategic about your referrals. Everyone has strengths. There is a web developer, Cynthia Lay—The Butterfly Herder, who specializes in working with public speakers. She is our *go-to* when we meet a speaker. Learn the personalities and niches of your referral partners and be sure to factor these in when sending out business.
- Spread the wealth. If you give a client the names of three real estate brokers to interview, you can advise all three that you passed along their contact information.
- Use social media. Follow referral partners on LinkedIn and Twitter and share their articles or comments. Promote them on your own social media business pages.
- Give them exposure. Our radio station is Star Worldwide Networks. During our Small Business Breakthrough Bootcamp, we always invite station manager Ed Vanderlee to come speak to our audience about the power of podcasting.
- Provide substantive information. Make yourself available to your referral partners. Offer to speak at their events. Ask if they need you to contribute to their newsletter. We have even done lunch-and-learns for them, talking about marketing improvement for their clients.

Four or five good referral partners can make a career for many of us; referral partners are critical to developing a business. Rather than targeting every prospect, it's more efficient to know the people who know the people you'd like to represent.

Keep in mind that quality is more important than quantity. You don't need dozens of referral partners to build your company; a few good partners can make a career. Focus on your best opportunities and concentrate your efforts on taking good care of them and their clients.

I hope you have noticed that throughout this chapter, I have publicly thanked lots of people who are our referral partners. You can do that, too! If you want to learn how, please reach out to us at www.FreeMarketingConsultation.

com. We will invest thirty-minutes of time together and, who knows, perhaps we will become referral partners!

47

Create More Sales in the Neighborhood

Would you like to take advantage of a conversation I had that will help build your business? The conversation occurred before seven o'clock in the morning, prior to when our weekly networking group began. It helped two very successful business owners with over more than fifty years of experience create more opportunities for sales.

Here's how it all came about. While we were all pouring our coffee, the realtor in our group was talking to the painter about his new truck and asked if he was going to put his company name on it. He replied that he was not sure, because in over thirty years, he had only had a couple calls ever from someone seeing his truck.

I added that he should check on the insurance, because lettering on the vehicle could cause it to be considered a commercial vehicle raising his rates.

The tree service member chimed in and said that it was worth it because he got calls *all* the time from his truck. It struck me in that moment how we were masterminding on a topic only up to the point of knowledge we had—no guessing was taking place.

From there, the conversation branched out and I asked both the tree-service person and the painter if they would like a marketing tip that would not matter what they had on their trucks. "Do you," I asked, "put a sign out front of the homes you work at?" Both nodded in the affirmative. "It's good to get that easy referral business, right?" I said.

Then I gave them an idea that I am sharing with you as well. If you are a contractor-type business that is working in homes, you should leave flyers at each home in the neighborhood two days prior to being there.

If I were to pause for a moment and ask you what should be on the flyer, most people would say it would be an ad for the company saying that "as long as we are here, we could do work for you, too."

Good thought but let's make it more valuable to the people in the neighborhood. Here is what that flyer *should* say:

Dear neighbors. Well, we are not *always* your neighbor. But on (*date* to *date*) we will be your neighbor because we are doing (*type of work*) at (*address*). It is our goal and desire to be an incredible neighbor to you while we are here. You will see our trucks on your street. If you have any inconvenience with our trucks, if they are in your way or my crew is not courteous, here is my cell phone number (*number*). *Please* call me immediately and I will solve the issue. We're looking forward to moving in for a few days. Best, (*your name*)

I would make the flyer look like your letter head. If you can handwrite it *neatly* and photocopy it, even better.

Your job is to be a good neighbor to the community that you are joining. *Their* job is to have a positive opinion of you.

Here are the caveats: If your phone rings you better pick it up. Fast. And if it is a problem, you better fix it. Fast. Your crew must know that these flyers are being put out and they are being watched by everyone in the neighborhood.

Here is another one: you are going to want to add a flyer that talks about you and your service and that they can call you and you give them a free estimate, *etc.* Don't do it. If they want you, they will call you.

Here is how you get around it. At the *end* of the time in the neighborhood, you can put out a *thank-you* note—"we loved being part of your neighbor" flyer. On the *other* side of that flyer, you can put your information.

Here is what is so great about this marketing tactic. It takes *zero* technology greater than a photocopier. You could literally handwrite the entire thing (*if your penmanship is spectacular*) and then make copies.

Here is what *else* is so great about this marketing tactic. It's *very* inexpensive. Ten or so flyers times two flyers per house is *twenty* flyers. At ten cents a flyer, for two dollars you get to make a very positive impression in a neighborhood where you already have work.

At the beginning of this chapter, I mentioned the number of years they had been in business because when we speak on stage, in front of small groups or full theaters with hundreds of people, we *always* have someone in our audience that says they know all about marketing for their industry because they have done it forever. This is an example of two guys who could have said "no thanks" when I asked them if they would like a marketing tip that would help them get more business immediately. I applaud business owners who take that point of view. In fact, quite often, some of our most successful private business coaching clients are the people who have been in their industry for a long time and understand what it is going to take to excel and get to that next level of achievement. Heck, our combined time in human resources, sales, and marketing totals several decades and *we* still have coaches for three different areas of our business.

Another example of this is when Francesco Molinari accepted the trophy for the British Open in 2018. The very first people he thanked were his multitude of coaches. Hey, if it's good enough for him, it's certainly good enough for us.

We would love to help you just like we helped these two business owners in our networking group. For your free thirty-minute marketing help, go to www.FreeMarketingConsultation.com . Take the quick assessment, click on our calendar and we can begin our conversation. We guarantee that in that consultation, we will give you at least one game changer, just like these two business owners received.

48

How to Start Promoting Your Business from Scratch

We wanted to share some tips on how to start promoting your business, because we get asked *all* the time what we would do if you were starting all over. It's an interesting question because when we start working with you, if feels like we are starting over because we are hopping on the marketing freeway all the way to the success circle. I absolutely get it. I have been there.

I have had to start from the beginning several times. First in college, working as a sales rep for my college newspaper, *The Daily Aztec*. After that it was for *The PennySaver*, selling direct mail shopper advertising. Then I completely changed from publications to promotional products which was followed by blending marketing help into the mix and the last time was leaving an area of Los Angeles where Sharyn and I were quite anchored, to move to Arizona to deeper develop that marketing coaching business, which is really a business coaching business because we cover far more than marketing.

How *would* I start over? It has not been so long ago, so I followed a formula.

1. Decide on demographics. That is who you want to work with the most, who you serve the most. The mistake here is that most entrepreneurs who are told to go through this exercise, are not told that there are probably more than one or two or even three demographic target markets for each business.

2. Create the proper messages. Where most entrepreneurs are misled is that they are told that the messages are advertisements, but they forget something very important. Those messages include helpful content. Most of the advertising tactics that are sold by salespeople are designed to attract someone with specials or features and sometimes benefits. I know because that used to be me.

3. Go to where those demographic business owners are playing. Those

same tactics that are described above could be the right place for you to place your messages. You will be able to figure out where they are playing if you pay attention to properly creating the messages. You are going to be out there in the marketplace of ideas hearing and seeing lots of methods. Here is a super-secret ninja marketing tip for you. Many of them use the phrase "it really gets your name out there." Always ask them specifically how. How has it worked for others just like you? How *will* your networking group benefit me? Who are the other members? Do they talk about needing my services? Ask the questions and listen to the answers.

4. Begin to build a list. The other three steps will be something you revisit on a quarterly basis, but this step is where the rubber meets the road and is a daily activity. We are always looking for people who want to connect with us. Here is an example. Through one of the social media platforms, Sharyn was contacted by a professional in the Pacific Northwest. That is not our main geographic area, but for us, geography is not one of the most important demographics. Her occupation and age were what makes us most likely to help her. She is coming to our next Small Business Breakthrough Bootcamp and we will continue that conversation.

5. Share those messages to the target markets. How did Sharyn get that conversation started with the potential new client? She is constantly putting our messages into the marketplaces where we know our clients are looking. Like number four, this is a never-ending process.

So that is how we would, and *have* begun from scratch, and will continue to do so. Would you like some help to get this done for you and your business? Let's have a conversation. Go to www.FreeMarketingConsultation.com and take the short assessment. You can go right into our calendar and we will get started.

49

Not Enough Evidence to Convict

Or, the ultimate thirty-minute sales symposium for people that weren't trained as salespeople.

The title of this final chapter is the title of a presentation that we are creating to add to our public speaking list of topics. The title comes from my long-held belief that if most salespeople were arrested and accused of being a salesperson, sadly there is not enough evidence to convict them. Since this is a sales book, it's kind of the law that there must be rules for salespeople. So, here are mine.

Many people call themselves marketers for a company. Their job is to be out in the community, telling the company's story and attempting to rustle up sales for their company. They take the title of marketing because they are reticent to admit that they are in sales. They want a salary instead of commission. Interestingly, most of you are probably entrepreneurs. You only make money if you sell something. You are in sales, but your people don't always want to admit that *they* are in sales. Heck, your receptionist is in sales. Each time he answers the phone, he can be the difference between a successful interaction for your company and a tragic failure because the call was handled poorly or unprofessionally.

The difference between marketing and sales is that marketing is getting them to raise their hands, sales is putting a pen in their hand and, if it's a good deal for both of you, getting them to use it.

Rule 1—You can't sell someone something they don't want.
Rule 1 corollary— at least you won't more than once.

If you have ever tried a McDonalds McRib sandwich, you either love it or hate it. And no amount of their advertising will change that. Years ago, when I was in the market for a stereo, the salesman introduced me to the brand name Rotel. I love getting brands that are different, did not want what was the most popular at the time, so he was able to get me to buy it because there were features that I really wanted. And still do. My turntable, however, was an easy choice because the Techniques SL-D2 was, and still is an amazing machine.

Rule 2—You must be prepared to sell your prospect the way they want to be sold.
Rule 2 Corollary—There are many ways to connect with your prospects.
Prior to our Small Business Breakthrough Bootcamps, we speak to many groups and talk about the event. When you decide to attend, you are reminded that you are attending because you have received emails, you have received snail mails, some of you even receive phone calls. Then at our bootcamps, you get to see us speak again. We told you about our blogs, our radio shows, our books. We want to connect with our potential clients and referral partners in whatever manner they want to receive the information. In other words, don't just rely on emails to do the job. Don't rely on *any* one method of connection to get the job done.

Rule 3—You must know what is different about you and your product compared to your competitors.
Rule 3 corollary—I'm not talking about features.
It is amazing that when I go to networking meetings how many people highlight their elevator speeches by saying that they have great service and great prices. Do you know *anyone* who says their service sucks and they are way too expensive? *No!* Service and price are *not* the ways to show how you stand out from the crowd. We know that there are other business coaches. But more than 95% of them are solo acts. We give our clients double the points of view and double the life experiences to build their business in sales, human resources, marketing, and public speaking. Most coaches focus on one of those. Advantage: Yuloff.
You can do the same thing. And if you want assistance, we will help you. Go to www.FreeMarketingConsultation.com.

Rule 4 —You must be ready for their responses.
Rule 4 corollary—some people will say *no.*
Some people will say *no* because even though the price is great, they want to do it themselves. Some will say *hell yes* let's get to the next level *now.* Some will say maybe—I have a couple of questions like can I make three payments instead of one. Some will say maybe—can my year-long program start May 1

instead of next week? We'll say yes, put a down payment down so you get the best price and we will start you with our online product.

We always say that *yes* is okay, and *no* is okay. It's the *maybe* or *later* or *I have to ask my dog groomer's spouse's nephew* that is hard to deal with. Let your potential client know that *no* is a perfectly acceptable answer.

Rule 5—If someone says no, don't be a jerk.
Most of you don't like salespeople or the concept of salespeople because some woman just kept pushing and pushing and calling and calling and lived by the rule "Keep selling until they buy or die."

Rule 5 corollary—but you must follow up.
- The average sale is made in contact number five to twelve.
- Most sales people only follow up once.
- Only a few follow up more than three times.

One of our favorite past times used to be going to time-share presentations, because they are just so awesome. It's a great product and the benefits are numerous. The downside is that you can *always* find someone re-selling their timeshare on the internet for a dollar if you take over the homeowners' association fees.

The last time we went to a presentation, we told the salesperson we were only there for the prizes. He said, "Okay," and continued to sell us. And sell us. And sell us . . . .

Until I finally *did* get it through to him that though I loved his sales pitch, we were not buying. He then became rude and stalked off in a huff, leaving us there at his desk. We had to go *find* the person who would give us our prize. Poorly done.

So, follow up the appropriate number of times, and don't let anyone be a jerk to you.

Your Lagniappe Bonus

There is nothing better for you, the salesperson, to give your clients than a little something extra that they don't expect. There is a French term I learned from a hotel manager years ago that describes this gift called *lagniappe.*

Merriam-Webster defines *lagniappe* this way: (lan-'yap) A small gift given to a customer by a merchant at the time of a purchase. Broadly this means something given or obtained gratuitously or by way of good measure. "The waiter added a cup of lobster bisque as a *lagniappe* to the meal."

So, here is your lagniappe. As a *thank you* for buying, reading, positively reviewing and sharing this book, we have created a bonus section for you called The Basic 15.

The section is based on one of our public speaking topics for large and small groups of small businesses where we describe the fifteen basic things you need to be doing in your marketing.

Your Lagniappe is waiting for you. It is at YuloffCreative.com/Lagniappe.

Thank you so very much for investing in our books, programs, and coaching. We look forward to working with you.

Bonus Appendix I

Yuloff Creative Interviewed by ABC's Secret Millionaire

An interview by James Malinchak with Hank and Sharyn

Jim: Hi this is James Malinchak, featured on ABC's hit TV show *Secret Millionaire*, and welcome. I'm so excited for my amazing interview today with two great people, Sharyn and Hank Yuloff. Hey guys, how are you? Welcome.

Sharyn: Thank you. Thanks for having us.

Hank: Good to meet you.

Jim: Glad to have you. So, folks are watching and why don't you explain exactly what it is that ya'll do?

Hank: We're business coaches, and whatever box people put that in, but we work on their marketing, because of Sharyn's background of fifteen years in HR, so we work on their human resources. And we're there as their backup. One of our clients said the other day said that we're the ones that she trusts to take her by the hand down the yellow-brick business path. So, I guess we are Dorothy and Toto.

Jim: (laughing) She's Dorothy and you're Toto.

Hank: Yeah, keeping you away from the flying monkeys.

Sharyn: Well we have other clients that call us their business incubator. So, we take them from where they are, and we add some amazing ingredients and get them really cooking.

Hank: So, you kind of like look at the whole gamut, I assume you go here's where you are. Here are your goals, your dreams, your visions of where you want to be. And you kind of try to provide them with that bridge or roadmap and it's probably different for everybody, right?

Sharyn: It is. I mean there are some similarities, of course. But yeah it is different for each business because their dreams and their goals are different.

141

Hank:	We start, we don't have one particular plan. They always say, what does it look like? What do you do? Well, it kind of depends, who do you want to work with? And we find out, like Sharyn said, what are their hopes, their dreams? What do they want their life to look like? And when we find out what they want their life to look like, then we go about the basic business stuff. Okay, your target market and where to find them, and then we work on messages and the right tactics. But most people do ask us when they meet us and say what they do, well, do you do social media? Well, it depends. So, it really is a conversation.
Jim:	It's not a one size fits all.
Sharyn:	It is not.
Hank:	It can't be.
Sharyn:	It's a path.
Jim:	So, why are you so passionate about this?
Hank:	You know, going back to college time, my first job in advertising I was working for my college newspaper. And I realized at twenty-one there were business owners that were asking my opinion about their business. So, for a very long time now I've been working with businesses that they're so in the trenches, they're so focused on the day to day stuff that they don't have a chance to look at the big picture. And we're there to help them out of the trench, to give them a couple of hands, to get them out and to get them on the right path.
Sharyn:	There is really nothing as exciting as watching a business owner come to us. And they have a vision for what they want, life to look like and we help them to create that business to create that life that they want. But then to actually get them to live that life is just, that's magical.
Hank:	Most people that are watching this, we all have blinders on for our own business. That's what we've found.
Jim:	That sounds right, yeah.
Hank:	Most of our clients, they have them for us. That's why we have coaches.
Jim:	You're too far into the forest that you don't see the trees.
Hank:	Absolutely. So, our job is to help them get the blinders off and get focused. That's when we see them when it just clicks, that's when it just rocks for us. We love that.
Sharyn:	That's right.
Jim:	Okay, I'm going to put you on the spot.

Hank:	Okay.
Jim:	There are a lot of business coaches out there. So other than obviously you get two of you, the dynamic duo, what makes you different?
Sharyn:	Well that's part of what makes us different, right?
Hank:	The dynamic duo.
Jim:	I love it.
Hank:	Yeah, there are so many, when you have a coach it's just them. You get their expertise, whatever they've learned along that path. With us you do get two of us with two different backgrounds with two different expertise that we then get to help our clients with the gamut of marketing, sales, human resources.
Jim:	I love that. You're kind of like the outside guy, right, the marketing, the sales. You're like the operations, HR and let's get this thing smoothly running. I mean it's the inside outside duo.
Hank:	Sometimes we'll get a call, we have an HR question. Sharyn. Well I'm not going to jump in. I was a sales manager for a company for a long while, but I didn't have, when I had an HR issue I had an HR department, so have Sharyn do that. When it's a sales question I tend to get it. When its messaging, we both dip our hands in there and work for both of them and make it work that way. A wise man told us, that we work for them, create for them, think for them and help them figure it all out.
Jim:	I love that. I love that. So, let's think about your clients you've had over the years, right. You've probably noticed that there's some common pitfalls, or common challenges or roadblocks that may stop them or hinder them. You've probably seen a few common ones. So, what are some of those? Those challenges that hold them back.
Hank:	Sometimes, it's, it's silly. Like, oh, I want to do this. Why? Well my friend has a business and it worked for him. Are they the same business? No, but hmm. So, okay, let's back it up and look. Or, again, they are so busy, you know.
Sharyn:	So many business owners were really taught how to do what they do, but they weren't taught how to market what they do. And that's what we're there for to help them then market what they do.
Hank:	Like, we have some clients who are lawyers. And there is no class in law school on how to market your practice.
Jim:	That's true.
Hank:	We have dentists who are clients. There's no class in dental school on

how to market your business. And it goes down the road. Every specialty, and we work with a lot of different ones. There's not classes. Unless they were thinking ahead and in college, you know, we're not thinking ahead. Take a marketing class. So that's our job. We're the marketing department down the hall or the HR department down the hall. They can pick up the phone and they can call us, and we work with them. We speak every week with our clients, and we make sure they're focused.

Sharyn: Are they on the right path? Did they veer off by accident and do we need to do a course correction?

Jim: And I would assume the more they grow or step into where they want to be, they have different challenges that pop up. They are always changing and adjusting. So, someone is watching, and they are thinking of maybe working with you. I want you to talk to that person. And I want you to tell them why they should work with you guys.

Hank: Because we're good.

Jim: You know, other than the fact that you guys are great.

Hank: Actually, they should try us out.

Jim: Oh, I like that.

Hank: Let's have a conversation. If you go to FreeMarketingConsultation.com, because that's what they're going to get. You see we like to keep it very simple. If you would like a free marketing consultation, and they can talk about HR, go to that website FreeMarketingConsultation.com. There is a very short, easy, simple intake form. And then you can go right into our calendar, and we'll talk. And we always say that we guarantee they are going have, we are going to be able to give them something that's going to help them.

Sharyn: Absolutely. At least one actionable tip that you can walk away with today.

Hank: And what happens a lot of times, we do marketing boot camps. And quite a few of our clients want to go to our boot camps and try us out.

Jim: Sure.

Hank: Come for two and a half days and we will show you how to market your business. And we have another conversation, if we're the right ones. Because honestly, we want to make sure it works both ways.

Jim: I love that. Why should thy work with you? Well, just try us out and you will see. I love it. It's so great.

Sharyn: It's the best way to know, right? Because if you are working with a coach, it has to be the right fit. If it's not the right fit, then they are not the right coach for you.

Jim: Sure.

Sharyn: So, test us out and see if we're the right fit.

Hank: If you go to our website there's tons of blog material. You will get an idea of how we work. In fact, you can go to our radio show. What is the radio show?

Sharyn: *The Marketing Checklist.*

Hank: There we go, *The Marketing Checklist.* There's a couple of hundred hours of us, sharing marketing tips and tricks. So, you can get an idea if we're the right ones for you pretty quickly.

Jim: So, there you have it. If you want to take your business to the next level, if you want to have a HR, and marketing department, around the corner, down the hall, across the street. These are the two you should work with. So, give them a call today or go to the website and have a conversation with them. You will be so grateful you did. I'm James Malinchak. Thanks for watching.

Bonus Appendix 2
Yuloff Creative Interviewed by Kevin Harrington of *Shark Tank*
An interview by Kevin Harrington with Hank and Sharyn

Kevin: Hi, I'm Kevin Harrington an original shark from the hit TV show *Shark Tank* and I'm here with Hank and Sharyn Yuloff. Hey guys how you doing?

Sharyn: Thanks for having us on the show.

Hank: So glad to be here.

Kevin: Good, good to have you. Hey now you wrote the book *The Marketing Checklist* and it's a series of books on marketing but let the folks that are out there listening right now tell us a little bit about your kind of marketing and what the book involves I know there's forty-nine steps I think in this version, so tell me about it.

Hank: It started this way: I wrote a book about business cards and I showed it to my coach and he said well you just told them forty-nine ways that they blew writing their business cards so where's the workbook. (*augh*)

Kevin: (chuckle)

Hank: So, I started putting another book together, okay they're going to need to know a little bit on marketing and all these different things and it turned out to be *The Marketing Checklist: 80 Simple Ways to Master Your Marketing.*

Kevin: (*umm*)

Hank: And I showed that to my coach proudly, hey look Amazon bestseller. Proudly busting my buttons.

Kevin: (chuckles) There you go, right.

Sharyn: (chuckles)

Hank: And he looked at me and said that's nice you still owe me a workbook for the first half. Oops.

Sharyn: Oops.

Kevin: (chuckles)

Hank: So, I went back and started writing more and it turned out it was at just another book and here is the marketing tip: if you know you're going to write more than one book, the eighty would have probably been sixty and that would have been about sixty.

Kevin: I got you, okay (chuckles).

Hank: Yeah so, and we're just now coming up with the third one which is a social media book the how's and whys of social media.

Kevin: (umhum)

Hank: And that includes a year's worth of social media content and I think we did what a six-hour training? (Asking question to Sharyn.)

Sharyn: Yes.

Hank: Yeah, a six-hour video training that goes with it just for buying the book. You get access to that.

Kevin: So, I know husband-and-wife team, been together thirty years the two of you that's amazing.

Hank: It's awesome, it's the *best.*

Sharyn: (chuckles with delight)

Kevin: That creates a passion, right, for your life and for business and help-ing other businesspeople and that's exciting, and I think that prob-ably exudes into helping people on a day to day basis, right?

Hank: Uh, huh.

Kevin: So, what I love about your story though is that and there's a lot of advertising agencies out there. The more they spend the more they make to get a percentage of all that. You guys are, you become like an in-house agency for small business owners, correct?

Sharyn: Correct.

Kevin: That's kind of the niche that you feel, and I think, I think it's a bril-liant idea. I love it, so yeah.

Hank: We're the marketing department down the hall.

Kevin: Right.

HANK: Most businesses would like a marketing department and they can virtually knock on our door.

Kevin: Yeah.

Sharyn: Yeah, were accessible via email and text and phone calls for all your urgencies.

Kevin: And so, because I always like to say what makes you different, but it's the differentiator here is that you're pretty much available on call like a you know twelve, eighteen hours a day almost, right? And then you go across all the spectrums, because the small business owner doesn't generally just use one thing he's got to have a little kind of dabble, a little bit in multiple things. But they're going to have to be very careful not to overdo it. So, you're thinking just almost as if you're the owners partner kind of right mentality as like this internal kind of thought processor of their plans.

Hank: Yeah, lets them know how we start with them.

Kevin: Yeah.

Hank: You go ahead, you go ahead, see we've been together so long we try and make sure the other one speaks enough.

Kevin: Okay.

Sharyn: We start with a two-day intensive at our marketing retreat property in Sedona, Arizona.

Kevin: Nice, beautiful place to come and have a retreat I think.

Sharyn: Its awesome.

Kevin: Yeah, great.

Sharyn: So yeah, we get to spend two days with them getting them, getting us first clear on what their goals are, then getting them started on the marketing path right, we follow up.

Kevin: And I know you work across many kinds of businesses we talked, you work with lawyers, you work with doctors, you work with heating and air conditioning companies.

Sharyn: We do.

Hank: Yeah as a matter of fact we do.

Kevin: How about that right?

Hank: We even have a magician.

Kevin: Oh, wow.

Hank: So, our company, when you come to our marketing boot camp, you get to see our official magician, Glenn Dolf. The magician is our official company magician.

Kevin: That is amazing, right?

Hank: Hey, how many, how many events can you go to where you get a magician to help your marketing.

Kevin: Hey, by the way they need marketing.

Hank: They do, that's funny. I mean, hey, some of the, I mean if you look at some of these magicians that are kind of famous, they put a marketing program together.

Sharyn: Absolutely.

Kevin: At some point that they followed and executed, and became you

149

know successful in a process right?

Hank: Most of our business though, they're the let's just think more normal or regular.

Kevin: Right.

Hank: One of our clients, her name's Angie, she owns a ten-location.

Sharyn: Transitional housing.

Hank: Yeah.

Kevin: Transitional housing, right.

Hank: When she came to Sedona when we were working together she said you know I've learned more from you in the first day than I have in twenty years of marketing my business.

Kevin: That's great.

Hank: We know there's a need.

Kevin: Yeah.

Hank: And, we try and help, you know, you the small business owner, we're trying to help small business owners find out, you know, how to put their name, the right message in front of the right people at the right time.

Kevin: Yeah so, this brings me to the question that what kinds of obstacles are many of these small business owners facing day to day right now. And how do you help them overcome those obstacles? What are some of the things happening in small business today?

Sharyn: Many small businesses, they don't know where to start. They don't know where to start to build their entrepreneurial dream.

Kevin: Right.

Sharyn: Or, they don't know where to start on their marketing path.

Kevin: Okay.

Sharyn: Or, now they've gotten a little bit bigger and they're starting to hire, and they don't know how to hire.

Kevin: Okay.

Sharyn: And luckily, I have over fifteen years of HR experience. So, part of what makes us unique is we get to help them focus on marketing sales and human resources.

Kevin: Okay.

Hank: So, we act as their business coach you know, we talk to them, we say we emphasize in marketing, HR, and sales.

Kevin: Right.

Hank: My background originally was from sales.

Kevin: Yeah.

Hank:	We're able to help them in a lot of diverse ways.
Kevin:	And you're not you're not afraid to bring in someone that's smart to help them in this area. Because that they now are working with you to help supercharge that business, so this is, so that's a true mentor and coach that is really looking out for the best interest of their clients, right?
Sharyn:	Absolutely.
Kevin:	Others might say, oh, I don't want any with too smart in there we may lose our job or something right, but you know.
Sharyn:	Its always what's in your best interest.
Kevin:	Yeah.
Hank:	Even, and some of our clients that have one of our clients, is a law firm and they have a marketing, what they call marketing person, it's really sales, I guess.
Kevin:	Right.
Hank:	And our job is to help and get her level up.
Kevin:	Yeah.
Hank:	So that they're marketing the firm.
Kevin:	You know sounds like big-brother marketing. Okay I mean it's like, it's like you act like a big brother to help them build their business. But what is the name of your company because I know the book says marketing.
Hank:	It's Yuloff Creative Marketing Solutions.
Kevin:	Yuloff Creative Marketing.
Hank:	The condensed version is Yuloff Creative.
Kevin:	Yuloff Creative, okay so and now after human resources for several years and sales join forces now. Coaching, mentoring, marketing etc. The books have been, you know, very cool for you to get out there, get a little buzz going, and so where does your business go from here? What's the next couple of years entail?
Hank:	We just launched in an online marketing program.
Kevin:	Okay.
Hank:	Because, you know, there are some businesses that aren't ready, you know, you're not ready to hire us yet. You're for whatever reason.
Kevin:	Okay.
Hank:	So, we have a program called the small business marketing plan, it's the smallbusinessmarketingplan.com, you know, it's right. What do you name it? Well, our target market is small businesses and what are we doing, we're giving a marketing plan, so there's the name.

Kevin:	Okay.
Hank:	Brilliant marketing, huh?
Kevin:	I like that. Keep it simple.
Sharyn:	So, when you have access to dozens and dozens of hours of us training, you get an action guide, and you can put its do-it-yourself marketing, plus they get a private Facebook group, and we do weekly dialing calls so when you buy that program you're not, you're not on your own.
Kevin:	Yeah.
Hank:	Because, you know, a lot of people, you'll buy a book.
Kevin:	Yeah.
Hank:	Or something, oh I'm so happy I bought this book.
Kevin:	Yeah.
Hank:	And it goes on the shelf.
Kevin:	Right.
Hank:	You're meaning to read it.
Kevin:	Yeah.
Hank:	Becomes what's it called—shelf help.
Kevin:	Yeah, shelf help, exactly.
Hank:	And we don't want that to be.
Kevin	Yeah.
Hank:	That's not us.
Kevin:	Yeah.
Hank:	We don't want to just sell somebody something.
Kevin:	Right.
Hank:	So, we put the program together and they get to come into the Facebook group and Sharyn, and I answer questions.
Kevin:	Yeah.
Hank:	As they go through.
Kevin:	I love, you know, so whether it's mentoring, coaching, or kind of a starter plan that you can put them in. You guys offer or it sounds like all the kind of options, you know, it's kind of step in. I like the option to spending two days in Sedona though.
Sharyn:	It's our favorite place too.
Kevin:	It's not a bad place to hang out.
Hank:	Its red rocks all the way around the hills, I love it.
Kevin:	I'm looking forward to seeing, I'm going to come see you sometime soon.
Sharyn:	I can't wait.

Hank: We'll play golf.

Kevin: Yeah, okay, one last question, okay. There's someone out there that's thinking I'm a small entrepreneur, medium size I may need a moment, maybe I should call Yuloff Creative and any words of encouragement for them right now to close out our segment?

Sharyn: You got this, you can do this. You're not alone. There are folks there that can help, and you should find those mentors that resonate with you that you have access to.

Kevin: Yeah.

Hank: I like to say that if ever, if things happen for a reason, we want you to be the reason things happen. And things do happen in business but keep moving forward and umm you know. Can we off give them one offer?

Kevin: Yes, sure please do.

Hank: If you find you're a little bit stuck and you just want that little bit of push you can get Sharyn and I on the phone for a half hour. If you go to free marketing consultation. Again, keep it simple. What are we doing? We're giving him a free marketing consultation. If you go to freemarketingconsultation.com you fill out a short easy form. You can go right into our calendar you'll get us on the phone for a half hour and we'll help you get focused and get some breakthrough and get you going.

Kevin: Hey thirty years together there's some wisdom going on here, okay. So, Sedona you got to check this out. Freemarketingconsultation. com and Hank and Sharyn Yuloff, Yuloff Creative, you guys are amazing.

Hank: Thanks for having us on.

Kevin: See you in Sedona, and you should also make that email right now, thanks for being with us today.

About the Authors

Hank Yuloff

Hank Yuloff is a targeted-marketing tactician with over thirty years' experience keeping companies top-of-mind with their customers.

In high school, after winning a writing contest to attend a Beatrice Foods stockholders meeting as a field trip, Hank Yuloff was given a Cross pen and pencil set with the corporate logo as a remembrance. Years later that meeting continues to shape his career.

After graduating from San Diego State University with a degree in advertising and public relations he began his career working for two newspapers and then became a President's Club member for both a direct-mail company and a promotional-products company (he was also one of their sales managers) before opening Promotionally Minded, in 1997. They specialize in targeted marketing plans (under the SedonaMarketing.com brand), logo development, client retention and appreciation programs, and run a nationally recognized promotional products company (that pen, and pencil set the ball rolling). All these brands have been combined into the Yuloff Creative Marketing Solutions moniker.

He is the author of the three books on marketing. *The Marketing Checklist 2: 49 More Simple Ways to Master Your Marketing* became a best seller in seven categories on Amazon.com.

Hank and his wife of twenty-five years, Sharyn, host a weekly radio show with the same name, *The Marketing Checklist*.

They are very excited about opening a new branch of their company called Yuloff Creative Marketing Solutions Retreats. That company creates two types of two-and-a-half-day events: For partner-owned small businesses, they create custom marketing plans in a highly focused, one-on-one setting *and* they also host small-group marketing bootcamps in a mastermind setting for similar, major demographic entrepreneurs.

In the spring of 2016, Hank and Sharyn finished filming an entrepreneurial mini-series with Brian Tracy called *Living Your List.*

And he still has that pen and pencil set!

Sharyn Yuloff

Sharyn grew up hearing that she should do what she loves, and her first favorite thing was math. She was the kid that finished her homework early and skipped ahead to see what was next. She took this love of math and tried accounting, accepting a job as an assistant controller at an independent film distribution house and grew in that job to executive assistant to the CFO.

That position led her to become the human resources manager for an independent producer. She then moved into the same job at a financial services firm, and finally became the HR director for a 2D to 3D film-conversion studio.

She began to see a way to bring these real-life business organization skills to her husband's promotional products business, and her decades in HR to help his clients. They started a new division of Promotionally Minded that included online business management and HR consulting.

During those fifteen years in human resources, she had been handling a core marketing issue, mostly internal marketing—the company to its employees—but while hiring, it was also external marketing.

As more of their clients are also couples and entrepreneurs, she realized that she had truly come full circle. Yes, they are creating strategic marketing plans, but they are also teaching what they have learned and continue to learn every day, marketing strategies as well as business building and interpersonal relations.

Other Books by Naked Book Publishing

49 Stupid Things People Do with Business Cards . . .
And How to Fix Them

The Marketing Checklist
80 Simple Ways to Master Your Marketing

The Marketing Checklist 2
49 More Simple Ways to Master Your Marketing

The Marketing Checklist for Social Media Marketing
The Hows and Whys of Social Media

The Marketing Checklist for Human Resources
The Right Way to Hire, Cultivate, and Terminate Employees,
All While Improving Your Marketing

And more in the pipeline as well!